Soul Searching

A Girl's Guide to Finding Herself

To Dad, Mom, Scott, and Joni Mitchell.
—Sarah

Published by
Beyond Words Publishing, Inc.
20827 NW Cornell Road, Suite 500
Hillsboro, Oregon 97124
503-531-8700/1-800-284-9673

The information contained in this book is intended to be educational and not for diagnosis, prescription, or treatment of mental and/or physical health disorders whatsoever. This information should not replace competent medical and/or psychological care. The author and publisher are in no way liable for any use or misuse of the information.

ISBN: 1-58270-035-4

Editors: Michelle Roehm and Marianne Monson-Burton
Design: Andrea Boven / Boven Design Studio, Inc.
Diagrams: Emily Strelow
Proofreader: Laura Carlsmith

Printed in the United States of America
Distributed to the book trade by Publishers Group West

Library of Congress Cataloging-in-Publication Data

Stillman, Sarah, 1984-
 Soul Searching : a girl's guide to finding herself / written by Sarah Stillman ; illustrated by Susan Gross.
  p. cm.
 ISBN 1-58270-035-4 (pbk)
 1. Girls— Conduct of life— Juvenile literature. 2. Spiritual life— Juvenile literature. [1. Self-evaluation. 2. Conduct of life. 3. Youths' Writings.] I. Gross, Susan, 1960- II. Title.

BJ1651 .S85 2000
158'.0835'2— dc21   00-042906

The corporate mission of Beyond Words Publishing, Inc.:
Inspire to Integrity

Soul Searching

A Girl's Guide to Finding Herself

WRITTEN BY *Sarah Stillman*

ILLUSTRATED BY SUSAN GROSS

BEYOND
WORDS
Publishing
I N C

Table of Contents

A Note from the Author

A skinny, freckle-faced girl catches my attention as I scan the magazine rack at my local bookstore. She is probably eleven or twelve, but obviously trying to look older in her flared jeans and chunky high-heels. What gets me thinking is the glossy teen magazine she holds in her hand promising "Ten Ways to Get That Guy!" and "The Absolute Coolest Back-to-School Gear." I can tell this girl is searching for answers. But why does she hope to find them in the pages of a superficial magazine?

I know why. I know because I, too, looked for advice and approval in these magazines. I figured that if I could be a little bit prettier or own a few more stylish clothes, then I could be more popular, and therefore, happy. Of course, as time went on I realized that it doesn't really work like that. After studying dozens of articles that promised to make me attractive and irresistible, it dawned on me that I was the same old Sarah as before. If anything, I felt more dissatisfied with my life, my looks, and my social status than ever. Studies show that I was not alone: 70 percent of women feel worse about themselves after reading fashion magazines.

The reason for this is simple. Cosmetic companies, clothing designers, plastic surgeons, and a wide range of corporations benefit from our self-hatred. After all, the dieting industry rakes in profits of 33 billion dollars a year from our insecurities. The articles in fashion magazines are filled with promises, urging us to "Get the Body You Deserve" or "Discover the Secrets to Being Beautiful." But the truth is, the magazine creators aren't trying to help us, they are just trying to sell to us! As I found out the hard way, their promises are empty. I was ready to read something new . . . something intelligent.

With this desire in mind, I began my search for meaningful literature on my mother's book shelves. After sorting through piles of dusty novels and prehistoric text books, I finally found a title that intrigued me. It was called *Reviving Ophelia: Saving the Selves of Adolescent Girls*. The title instantly sparked my curiosity. I began to read, wondering if I needed saving and if this book could help. Instead, I found frightening passages such as this:

> *Girls today are much more oppressed. They are coming of age in a more dangerous, sexualized and media-saturated culture. They face incredible pressures to be beautiful and sophisticated, which in junior high means using chemicals and being sexual. As they navigate a more dangerous world, girls are less protected.*

The author, Dr. Mary Pipher, is convinced that adolescence is a painful and identity-shattering process for most young women. It made me wonder, *Are we really oppressed? Is this culture really as dangerous and media-saturated as Dr. Pipher suggests? If so, what should we do?*

I began paying attention to the signs that *Reviving Ophelia* wasn't exaggerating the difficulties most teens face: my good friend was bulimic, some of my schoolmates were using drugs, many of my phone conversations revolved around comforting a depressed bud. I listened to the facts on the news:

- 61 percent of girls report that they have dieted in the last year, but only eleven percent actually are overweight.
- 25 percent of girls suffer from some form of depression.
- In certain cities, the percentage of girls who have considered suicide is as high as 40 percent.

Along with the fear these statistics bought to mind came a question growing in importance: *What can we do about it?*

Well, I had already conducted a fruitless search for answers in teen magazines, so I knew they weren't the place to go. Instead, I roamed the library looking for a book on teenage "soul searching"—something that looked at the deeper subjects of self-exploration and spirituality for girls—yet I couldn't find a single book that addressed me as a teen today. I even conducted an Internet search with the words "spirituality for teenage girls"—only to receive a list of pornography sites!

That was the last straw. I knew something had to be written for girls who didn't want adolescence to get the best of them. And I figured, if someone needs to write it, why not me? After all, psychology experts like Dr. Mary Pipher can only analyze the needs of today's young women from afar. As a sixteen-year-old girl myself, I know what it's like to fear violence, drugs, and growing up. I understand the desire for popularity, beauty, and acceptance, thanks to first-hand experience. Most important, I know how great it feels to confront these things using self-discovery as my weapon.

Although it took me several years, I eventually learned to escape from the poisons of our culture by "soul searching." It began most intensely for me in seventh grade, a time when nightmares of being chased and falling were keeping me awake at night. I soon came across the idea of recording my dreams and learning to interpret the messages of my subconscious. Eventually, my dream journal became more than just a place to rehash my nightly visions; it developed into a venue for understanding my reality.

Using dream interpretation as my starting point, I first began exploring my spirituality. Ever since then, I've eagerly sought creative ways to follow my intuition and learn about myself. Each new tool I discovered, from meditation to feng shui, fueled my self-discovery mission. I came to realize that the more soul searching I did, the easier it became to cope with the problems in my life: betrayal from friends, expectations from parents, stressful situations at school, etc.

Each day now (Okay, I admit, I'm not *always* faithful!) I try to use journaling to vent my emotions, meditation to clear my mind, and yoga to calm my body. I still haven't conquered all of my nightmares and fears, of course, but I've certainly gotten closer. I want to share the tools I've found with girls around the world, because I think they can help us triumph over the destructive forces that books like *Reviving Ophelia* describe.

This book is completely unique. It is for girls who want to understand the true nature of who they are . . . for girls who love self-exploration, thinking, improving . . . for girls who desire happiness and are willing to actively seek it.

In the pages of *Soul Searching*, you can explore dozens of self-discovery techniques, from dream interpretation to volunteer work to aromatherapy. You'll take quizzes and use brainstorming activities to explore your inner wisdom. Of course, this book won't solve your problems or change your life immediately.

But if you are dedicated to self-understanding, *change will follow.*

You are setting out on a journey that is probably the most important one of your life. Just the fact that you are reading this book says that you understand the value of knowing your true self. As you read, I urge you to share what you learn with friends, discuss it with family, and work to apply it in your everyday life. I would love to hear from you about your experiences with this book and your own journey as a fellow soul searcher.

Best wishes,

Sarah Stillman
e-mail: soulsearch16@hotmail.com

CHAPTER 1

What is "Soul Searching"?

LOOKING WITHIN

". . . I can't explain how much it hurts to lose my spot of instant security in 'the group,' where I always felt comfortable and confident that someone would be standing next to me. It's so much easier when you and your friends are the same person, the same identity, going everywhere together . . ."

—MY DIARY, MAY 28, 1997

As my angst-ridden journal entries can testify, seventh grade was a tough year for me. Exclusive cliques and painful gossip were eating away at my self-esteem, forcing me into a state of questioning. Should I change myself, conform, in order to be popular and accepted? Was I a worthwhile person on my own, or did I need lots of friends to prove it? What was the value of being "cool," anyhow?

Unfortunately, it sometimes takes a painful situation to awaken our need for self-discovery. In my case, I was searching for a sense of inner worth in the wake of my peers' rejection. You probably have your own reasons for beginning this soul searching journey. Maybe you're also seeking self-acceptance after a difficult time. Or maybe you've been having a good time in life, yet you get the feeling there's more to it than that.

No matter what made each of us open the pages of this book, we've all got a similar challenge: we must learn to listen to ourselves. Once upon a time, this was a truly arduous undertaking for me. I was such an indecisive person that even the "simple" task of choosing an ice cream flavor took me ten minutes—on a *good* day. Often, I'd try to make my mom choose for me, or I'd point to my brother and say, "I'll have whatever he's having." But eventually, I learned to listen to what *I* wanted. I developed a system of closing my eyes, envisioning each flavor on my tongue, and rating the pleasure factor. All of a sudden, it was a million times easier to decide between vanilla ice cream and rocky road, a cake cone and a waffle cone, or rainbow sprinkles and Oreo chunks.

Sure, it may sound melodramatic to compare dessert choices to our inner journey, but learning to respect our own desires is no easy task. Thankfully, my middle school years taught me a lot about self-awareness. Similar to that spot inside my mind where I test hypothetical ice cream cones, I've developed a quiet place within for remembering who I am. It's the place I seek when I'm drowning in a moment of indecision, conflict, or discontent.

Certainly, we all know what's best for us inside—it's only a matter of listening. Soul searching is about tuning into this inner wisdom; with it, we can learn to harness our brilliance much like a radio antenna can make enchanting music out of invisible airwaves. Extending our antennas isn't hard to do. The techniques in this book, like journaling, yoga, and meditation, will help us. The first step, however, is inviting wisdom into our lives.

When you feel ready to begin your soul searching journey, take the following quiz. Find a quiet time and place before you start. Lunchtime at your school cafeteria will probably not be private enough to dig into your inner feelings! Think hard about each question and write your answers in a permanent place, such as a notebook, journal, or even in this book.

QUIZ: ALL ABOUT ME!!!

1. Tonight you will be offered a magic potion that will allow you to change one thing about yourself. Will you take it? If so, what will you change?

2. List ten things that bring you great joy (watching kung fu movies, riding your bike, playing with your puppy, etc.).

3. List five things you're confident about in your life (your ability to solve math problems, cracking jokes, painting, etc.).

4. List five things you're insecure about and why.

5. Think of someone you really admire. What is it about this person that makes him or her great? Do you share this quality?

6. Think of someone who annoys you, makes you mad, or hurts your feelings. Why do you think he or she has this effect on you? Do you ever make others feel the same way?

7. What do you like about the world and our society? Write down three things that give you hope. What bothers you the most about them? Write down three things you would like to change.

8. Write about the last time you cried. When was it, and why? Then write about the last time you felt deep emotion.

9. Think of three ways you are stereotyped, both positively and negatively. For each stereotype, write down a few reasons why it doesn't fit you. (For example, people might say you're brainy and a bookworm, but you also spend a lot of your free time hanging out with friends, playing basketball, etc.)

10. Write down ten words that best describe you. Your list can include adjectives, animals, objects, or colors—anything that represents your identity.

Now that you're done, review your answers. Have you ever thought about these things before? Exactly how familiar do you feel with yourself? Keep your answers close at hand and look back on them as you continue through the book. Some of your answers may change as you learn and grow, so don't be afraid to make adjustments to them.

UMMM. . .WHAT EXACTLY *IS* SOUL SEARCHING?

? Before we go any further, let's take a moment to understand what "soul searching" really is and why we should bother doing it. Whether you believe in the existence of a "soul" or not is beside the point. Even for people who don't, it's hard to deny the presence of an inner self separate from the image we project to the outside world. Just think of a time when you have felt that the "real you" was different from the way you acted around your friends, family, and acquaintances.

When we refer to soul searching, we're talking about the quest to become familiar with our inner voice, to understand it, and to follow it. A lack of internal communication is at the heart of many problems plaguing teenage girls: eating disorders, drug abuse, loneliness, low self-esteem. If we trust ourselves to begin with, it's much easier to resist negative media images and peer pressure. Soul searching also gives us:

- greater access to our creativity and intuition
- the confidence to follow our dreams
- better communication with our peers, family, and others
- a life of peace, purpose, and abundance

Along with these general benefits, many of the techniques you'll learn about in this book yield more explicit bonuses. They can:

- relieve stress, insomnia, and depression
- increase communication between the left and right hemispheres of the brain
- boost your mental clarity and physical energy

As you can see, soul searching is clearly worth the investment of our time and energy. And beyond the tangible mental and physical benefits, there is a great power that comes from knowing our inner voice intimately—of being able to use that voice to help us navigate our world confidently and calmly.

You have already begun to question by completing the "All About Me!" quiz, but there's still much, much more to ask. Living in America, we're used to quick results: microwaves, e-mail, hairdryers, ect. However, the attempt to find ourselves is no speedy mission—it's a perpetual search. Some people believe it's impossible to ever fully understand yourself completely. As Thoreau once said, "It's harder to know oneself than to look backwards without turning around." However, the mere process of trying will yield great results!

FINDING THE TIME

One of the largest barriers to soul searching is the lack of space we make for it in our busy lives. Probably every teen in the country feels like she or he has too many expectations and too little time! We're already spread so thin, between homework and guitar lessons, sports practice, and friends, where can we possibly find the time for soul searching?

Quite frankly, soul searching deserves a spot on your to-do list, no matter how crowded it may look. To say you can't find the time for soul searching is like saying, "I'm too busy driving to fill up my gas tank." Some things in life are investments. Although we give up time now for self-exploration, eventually we will receive the benefits that will make it worthwhile. For example, instead of spending hours stressing over an upcoming history test, meditation techniques will give us the mental focus to study more efficiently and effectively than ever.

So how can we find the time for soul searching in our lives? My first and foremost suggestion may be a little radical. It will take self-discipline and sacrifice. It will put you at risk for not being the most up-to-date girl in school. It will mean missing the season premiere of your favorite TV show, along with video games, music videos, and even news programs. I dare you to STOP WATCHING TELEVISION!!!

The Great TV Turn-Off

The more time we spend mesmerized in front of the tube, the more we give it permission to drain our spiritual energy and promote negative stereotypes. Although I admit we can't totally escape the media (nor do we necessarily want to), replacing our TV time with "soul searching" time is an easy way to bring tremendous change into our lives. The average person watches about 1,642 hours of TV each year—that means we'll watch over 82,000 hours between the ages of 13 and 63!!! That's about fourteen years of our waking lives lost forever to TV!

Imagine all of the wonderful things we could do with that time instead—we could really change the world! We could write novels . . . learn to speak Chinese . . . go scuba diving . . . dance the salsa! We could soul search! By taking the daring leap into the land of the TV-free, you'll add 5,125 days worth of extra time to your life that can be devoted to you, you, you! April 24-30 is National TV-Turn-Off week. Give it a try!

The Land of the TV-Free

Life without television isn't necessarily glamorous or exciting. In fact, you're likely to find it quite dif-

What do YOU think?

There are a lot of fun, positive TV programs out there, but personally, I think that most people—not just girls—can find better things to do with their time.
—JULIA HALPRIN JACKSON, AGE 16

While I don't think that TV is totally bad for girls, it isn't completely good either. It entertains while connecting girls to the world, and yet it can also cut girls off from the world while they are sitting on their couches. The entertainment itself is sometimes in question as well.
—EMMARIE HUETTEMAN, AGE 13

TV is bad because it projects horrible images and it makes you feel like buying stuff that you don't even need. If I could never watch TV again, I would do more outdoor things, like hiking.
—SOPHIE JEANNOT, AGE 16

I don't think TV is good for girls overall. It still drills in the old stereotypes of "blonde and thin equals pretty." If there were more shows with real girls (by real girls I mean girls with brains; even though she is a cartoon, Lisa Simpson is a good example) and not Barbie, it would increase girls' self-esteem.
—ANONYMOUS

Sitting down and watching something specific, I think is okay. What is destructive to girls is mindless surfing with no purpose. Then we are vulnerable to the destructive messages hidden inside television programs and commercials.
—CAITLIN DWYER, AGE 16

ficult at first. As Dr. Richard Carlson points out, "Much of our identity and inner struggle stem from our busy, overactive minds always needing something to entertain them." Thus, we rush to the TV set whenever we have a spare moment to fill, as if we're too frightened to confront the silence of our own minds.

When you first shut off your television, you'll probably be tempted to run from the stillness by picking up the telephone or grabbing a magazine. As busy teens, we're unaccustomed to quiet time, which we often label "boring." However, scientists studying human creativity have discovered that boredom is one of the best catalysts for our most original, exciting, and unique ideas. As an essential step in the creative process, it allows us to think in new, wacky ways that we normally wouldn't consider during life's daily hustle and bustle.

So, instead of feeling obligated to fill the silence following your TV turn-off, give your mind a brief moment of freedom. Sit, relax, and breathe deeply. Tell yourself, *Ahhh . . . I have nothing to do and nowhere to go.* After this rare respite, your mind will be in perfect shape for soul searching.

CREATING THE TIME

Cutting television out of our lives isn't the only way to find time for soul searching. It doesn't matter how we do it—as long as we do it! Prioritizing can help. Take a look at your daily routine and figure out how to make more "personal time" for yourself. Are you efficient about doing your homework or do you procrastinate? How much time do you spend getting dressed each morning, talking on the telephone, or worrying about school, boys, or whatever?

If you organize your time according to your priorities, there will always be room for the important things in life. How valuable is soul searching to you? Remember, no matter how busy things may seem, where there's a will, there's a way. If you don't put on that extra layer of make-up in the morning, you'll have an extra five minutes to write in your dream journal. If you do your homework when you get home from school instead of watching TV, you'll have extra time later on to paint or do yoga. Make every little moment count.

Also, soul searching isn't just about doing specific activities like visualization or feng shui. At its root, soul searching is a method of thought, a lifestyle. Surely, the act of writing, praying, or volunteering can move us in the right direction, but true soul searching transcends all words and actions. It is about entering a deeper place—a place where we are free from other people's desires or expectations and can follow what we truly love in our hearts.

How to Use This Book

There are various ways to approach this book. Since many different techniques are discussed, you may wish to skim through and jump in whenever a particular idea interests you. If you're one of those people who has a hard time reading a book from cover to cover, don't be afraid to skip around.

However, I suggest you move through this book from front to back, trying each activity as you go. The chapters progress methodically, starting with essential instructions on creating a calm space and relaxation, then moving on to more advanced ideas like meditation and philosophy.

This book will work best if you keep an open mind and experiment with as many techniques possible. After all, you never know which tools will suit you best. I personally rely most on my dream journal, but I know people who prefer art, visualization, volunteering, and the list goes on and on. Don't expect to enjoy every suggestion in this book—use those you enjoy most; make them work for you. The purpose of this book is to expose you to *many different* ideas so you can discover which tools will help *you* the most. At the end of each chapter there's a list of resources to help you find more information on the topics of most interest to you. All right, let's get started!

Resources

Big World, Small Screen: The Role of Television in American Society, by N. Feshbach, et al

Deadly Persuasion: Why Women and Girls Must Fight the Addictive Power of Advertising, by Jean Kilbourne

The 7 Habits of Highly Effective Teens, by Sean Covey

CHAPTER 2

Calm Your World

CREATING A SACRED SPACE THROUGH COLORS, FENG SHUI, AND AROMATHERAPY

Have you ever noticed how quickly your spirits are lifted when you arrive at a beautiful place like a waterfall or mountain? Or how quickly you get stressed out when you're sitting in a car, stuck in traffic? Our environment has a powerful effect over our minds. Because of the strong link between mind and matter, an important part of soul searching involves creating a space we love. Obviously, we won't have access to scenic beauty every time we want to relax. We must learn to make beauty out of what we have. In the process of making this space, we will have to discover what brings us joy and tranquillity. What colors, art, and objects reflect who we are?

Any space can become sacred, even if you live in a cramped apartment or share a room with your messy little sister. The techniques in this chapter will encourage you to bring your identity and your environment into touch with one another. The process of creating a spiritual space is important because in order for your space to reflect your identity, you'll have to do some soul searching.

Eventually, every place you go will become a home for soul searching. It really doesn't matter if you've got a full bedroom to yourself, a corner of the basement, or just your locker at school. As author Twylah Nitsch explains, "Each of us carries our sacred space within us, and our challenge is to live from it throughout our life's journey." To start, let's focus on one or two special places we can call our own.

CREATE A SOUL SEARCHING PLACE

When you were a little kid, did you have a favorite spot where you spent hours among the company of Legos, dolls, or picture books? I often built forts out of cushions in the living room or imagined I was the president in my clubhouse. Places like these are magical—the bathtub can serve as an underwater cave, or the closet can become a time-travel machine. Children are experts at making ordinary spots become beautiful. Although you probably don't build blanket forts anymore, using your creativity to transform your environment is a very healing and important thing to do.

As the renowned professor Joseph Campbell wrote, "You must have a room or a certain hour or so in a day, where you don't know what was in the newspapers that morning, you don't know who your friends are, you don't know what you owe anybody . . . . This is a place where you can simply experience and bring forth what you are and what you might be. This is a place of creative incubation. At first you may find that nothing happens there. But if you have a sacred place and use it, something eventually will happen."

Couldn't we all use a place like this? Maybe you already have one. Your bedroom might be your sanctuary, or you might have a favorite hammock, garden, or attic hideaway. In my opinion, sacred places should be havens for silence and solitude. If your family is really loud or you live in a crowded city, it may seem like a struggle to find a quiet spot. Instead of searching your house or apartment, maybe you could find a nice couch in the public library or a bench in the park. We don't necessarily need to be alone to have solitude. Even in the midst of commotion, we can learn how to focus our attention inward.

Check Out Your Space

There are lots of ways to transform your space. By paying attention to objects in your surroundings and how they make you feel, you can learn more about who you are, your likes, and your dislikes. When your space is filled with items that reflect who you are, you will feel pacified and motivated by that area.

Let's begin by thinking about bedrooms. Picture your bedroom right now, or go to it. Do you have any decorations on the walls? Posters taped to the ceiling? Are you surrounded by things you love. . .or by things that are supposed to impress your friends?

Continue asking yourself questions about your room and taking an inventory of your surroundings. It's often a surprise to realize the uninspiring images with which we fill our space. Many of my friends have walls plastered with supermodel photos and vodka ads. How can we consider a place sacred if it is saturated in negativity?

If it seems like your room needs a soul searching make-over, don't worry. There are lots of ways to perk things up. Begin by removing any objects in your room that don't communicate positive and accurate messages about yourself. It may be hard at first, but it will feel great to pull down anything that is distracting you from your true identity.

Make A "Soul Shrine"

Now that you've created some new space, you can use the extra room to create a Soul Shrine. Fill this space with things you love, successes, or great memories you've had, and dreams for the future. Begin by finding a small corner of your room that isn't being used, preferably one with a shelf, desk, or other space for objects to be displayed. Then gather small objects that are meaningful to you: your favorite seashell, a photo of a family vacation, a beautiful feather you found outside, a copy of your favorite prayer—whatever brings you comfort or makes you smile! Be sure to include things you're proud of as well: an award you won, a story you wrote, or a painting you created.

Design your Soul Shrine using the objects you've gathered. You may also wish to place incense, candles, or potpourri in your shrine. Go to this sacred space whenever you need an escape from reality. This is the perfect place to meditate, paint, or write in a journal, because it holds objects that will help you get in touch with your soul!

Another way to make your room more reflective of your personality is to make a mental list of all the things you value about yourself. Then, make sure your environment nurtures these things. For example, if you really take pride in your creativity, then make sure to hang your artwork on the wall or put a quote from your favorite musician beside your desk. Personally, literature and reading are a very important part of my life. When I was re-evaluating my room, I decided to copy my favorite quotes onto pieces of pastel construction paper and post them across from my bed. The quotes inspire me when I'm struggling with my own writing.

COLOR YOUR MOOD

Another way to assess your room is to examine the colors with which you surround yourself. Colors are an incredibly powerful part of our lives that are too often overlooked. Did you know there is actually a profession called color analysis, dedicated to helping people understand the effects of colors on our lives? Psychologists have discovered that the colors around us can really affect our feelings! In certain experiments, for example, they found that when prison cells were repainted in baby blue or pink, prisoners gradually became less aggressive, angry, and violent.

So when you're evaluating your space, use the power of colors to your advantage. Start brainstorming various ways to add a splash of color to your life. Some girls might have a room they're allowed to paint. Since painting a whole room is pretty time consuming, consider adding a border to the tops of your walls or little flourishes here and there. One of my friends painted her ceiling with a blue sky, white puffy clouds, and cute little birds! Her room is definitely a true reflection of her personality.

If painting is not your style, think about the other ways color infuses your life. Even changing the color of your bed sheets can be a way to express yourself. The following list is a guide to the most common colors and how we can use them to create our sacred space:

Yellow: Because it is cheerful, bright, and sunny, this color brings energy and optimism. It is a wonderful color for communicating joy and "inner sunshine."

Blue: This is the color of dreams, deep thoughts, and introspection. It is the perfect soul searching color! Light blue can express our gentle side, the home of our sensitivity and self-awareness.

Purple: Also known as the color of royalty, this shade is traditionally associated with people who are expressive, romantic, soulful, and creative. It can show our moodier, more intuitive side.

Green: Nature's strength and clarity of purpose is conveyed through this color. Because it is the shade of most healthy leaves and plants, it's a great color for lovers of Mother Earth and for well-focused, clear-headed girls.

Red: This hue is powerful, intense, and bold. Just like fire, girls who relate to red are often intense, outgoing, and passionate. Red is great when we need motivation or charisma.

Orange: Flamboyant and complex are words that color analysts often use to describe people who love this color. Many artists and actors are drawn to its dramatic and energetic vibe!

Pink: As I mentioned, this color has been proven to bring hope and alleviate aggression. It is a wonderful shade for affectionate and optimistic soul searchers.

FENG-WHAT?!

Feng shui (pronounced feng shway) is an ancient Chinese philosophy for using the energy of your surroundings to improve your life. Have you ever noticed that some places make you feel full of positive energy while others make you nervous or tired? For example, whenever I enter my dusty, cramped attic, I start to feel drained and exhausted. Why could this be? Well, feng shui believers say that the arrangement of objects and colors in a room affects you by encouraging or blocking the natural flow of energy.

So how can you put the forces of nature on your side when you're creating your sacred space?

Step 1: Clear out the clutter
Clutter and messiness in your room definitely encourage negative energy—they are a distraction to your soul searching.

Step 2: Find your "power objects"
There are many objects that feng shui followers believe will have a positive impact on your energy. These objects will immediately add powerful energy to any room. Also, objects you truly love will naturally help you feel positive energy when you are around them. Here are some traditional power objects:

Light: Candles, electric lights, fires, lava lamps, etc. Also, any objects that reflect light, such as mirrors, crystals, or shiny material such as tin foil.

Sounds: Pleasant noises like moving water, gentle music, singing birds, chimes, bells, and musical instruments. Anything that gives off appealing vibrations— even music boxes.

Colors: Paint, wallpaper, art work, even colored construction paper can make a huge impact on the energy of a room. Pay attention to how colors make you feel. Every color has its own mood, and the trick is to pick colors that encourage the mood you are trying to create. See the earlier color section for colors that reflect your personality and can increase positive energy flow.

Weight: Heavy objects like big rocks and statues, or pictures of heavy items such as a photograph of an elephant. Heavy objects give feelings of permanence, tranquillity, and solidity. Are you feeling like your life is a whirlwind? Surrounding yourself with heavy objects may help when you want to slow down.

Living things: Pets, from goldfish to kittens, as long as they are clean, healthy, and well cared for, can add positive energy. Plants give off tons of energy too, provided they are in good condition. Anything living invites growth, renewal, and vitality.

Moving objects: Mobiles, chimes, water (fountains are great!), fans, breezes, etc. Anything that moves makes your room a place that invites activity and accomplishment.

Step 3: Rearrange your room

Feng shui teaches that where you place objects in a room is just as important as the objects themselves. Each area in a room holds the energy for a different area of your life, so rearranging your room can change the energy flow in your room and your life.

Often, people use a feng shui map, like the one on the next page, to help arrange furniture and other objects. Each section on this octagonal-shaped map represents a different area in your life. By changing the arrangement of items within each section, feng shui believers say you can make improvements in that life area.

Stand in the doorway of your room and hold up the map so that the doorway on the map is facing the same direction you are. The feng shui map is divided into eight different life areas.

FENG SHUI MAP

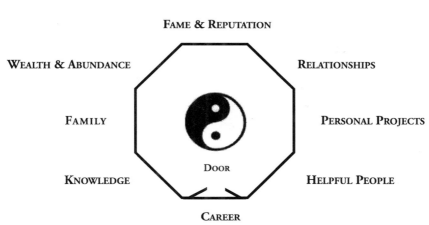

FAME & REPUTATION

WEALTH & ABUNDANCE

RELATIONSHIPS

FAMILY

PERSONAL PROJECTS

KNOWLEDGE

DOOR

HELPFUL PEOPLE

CAREER

There are many ways to enhance these areas of your life. Here are just a few suggestions:

Helpful people: Did you ever have a coach or teacher that did something special for you? A friend that helped you out when you were feeling down? This is the area to remember what people have done for you in the past and to encourage the help of others in the future. Anything that reminds you of these people, like a picture, an award, or a note, could be placed here.

Personal Projects: In traditional feng shui, this area represents children, but I feel it can also represent "projects" for most teenagers who don't have children. Are you working on a painting or needing help with a writing project? Place a power object in this area. White, silver, and gold are colors that encourage productivity in this life area.

Relationships: Why not put a vase of fresh flowers here to help your relationships bloom? You could also put up pictures of people you are close to (or want to be close to) and any objects or decorations that form a pair, like a set of candles or matching teacup and saucer. This will foster companionship.

Fame and Reputation: So, you want to be a famous actress? This area is for you. Try hanging pictures of birds in flight, the sun, the moon, and the stars—anything that symbolizes reaching for the sky!

Wealth and Abundance: To encourage abundance in your life, you could hang a crystal in this corner of your room or add a bowl of brightly-colored fish. A healthy green plant in this area may encourage your bank account to grow. Thinking of starting your own business? Red items are said to encourage prosperity.

Family: Are you having problems with your dad? Brother driving you crazy? Pay some attention to this area. Give it a good cleaning. Hang photos of your family or pets. You can also place here any cards, family heirlooms, or other objects that represent close relatives.

Knowledge: Try putting up a list of classes you want to improve in. To inspire even greater wisdom, why not put a bookshelf with books by your favorite authors in this area? While studying, keep your back to this wall to capture the flow of intellectual energy.

Career: Bells or chimes on a door can increase the flow of energy in your career area. Pictures or sculptures of leaping frogs can foster career growth and development. If you dream of becoming an astro- naut, stick up some glow-in-the-dark stars on this wall.

Mind the Door

One last tip to turn your room into a masterpiece of positive energy: door-ways are places of extremely high energy. Because of this, it is a good idea to place your desk in a way that you can face the door and receive the energy flow while you work—it should help you feel revitalized. For the same reason, put your bed as far from the door as possible. All that energy coming at you will stop you from getting a restful sleep. If you can't move your bed away from the door, hang a crystal between them so the crystal can block the energy flow and help you sleep!

HEALING AROMAS

Aromatherapy, the art of scent-related healing, is another way to positively impact our space. Aromatherapy has been around for over 5,000 years! The Egyptians loved perfumes, and sometimes concocted euphoric scents comprised of more than 60 ingredients. The ancient Greeks soaked in aromatic baths daily to prevent illness. Did you know the Bible makes reference to essential oils like frankincense, myrrh, and rosemary 188 times? By the turn of the eighteenth century, essential oils such as cinnamon and rosemary were being used to "preserveth visage and ye memory." And even now we can use these oils to affect our space and learn about ourselves.

Smell has a powerful ability to conjure up memories of people and places and to affect our mood. Can you recall the way your mother smells when you hug her? How do these smells make you feel: an ocean breeze, the air after a rain storm, cedars in a forest, or a sterile school classroom? Just as colors can affect the visual impact of a room, smells bring in an emotion as well. Believe it or not, we can learn about ourselves from the smells we are drawn to. And we can use smells to change the mood in a room quickly. Whether we want to energize ourselves or create a place of peace, aromatherapy has much to offer.

What do YOU think?

I relax by lighting candles and drawing or by writing poems.

—SOPHIE JEANNOT, AGE 16

On days when I've been on the go continuously, I just like to find something to do that includes sitting or lying down. I do anything from type on my computer while listening and singing along with a CD to reading a book in a warm bath. I like to use calming smells, like lavender, to feel more relaxed.

—EMMARIE HUETTEMAN, AGE 13

I relax by kicking target pads at Tae Kwon Do, writing poetry, taking bubble baths, and listening to soothing music.

—ASHLEY ROSEN, AGE 16

Fill Up Your Senses

There are hundreds of different smells around us every day. Each has its own personality and effect. To discover a scent's effect on you, close your eyes and breathe deeply. Try to pay attention to any pictures or emotions that the smell creates for you. Although scents have traditional effects they are associated with, the result will vary from person to person. Choose the scent that creates the mood you are seeking. Here are a few traditional associations for some common scents:

Chamomile: Releases fatigue and stress.

Jasmine: Relaxes, soothes, helps boost self-confidence.

Lavender: Restores balance, calms, or stimulates according to your needs.

Nutmeg: Promotes peaceful sleep with many dreams.

Orange: Calms, helps meditation, promotes cheerfulness.

Peppermint: Stimulates, refreshes, cools, and uplifts.

Rose: Encourages romantic and creative moods.

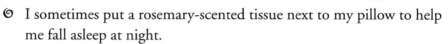

How To Use Aromas

There are lots of ways to use smells in our lives. Here are my favorite things to do with them:

- I sometimes put a rosemary-scented tissue next to my pillow to help me fall asleep at night.
- To freshen up the scent of my room, I put a drop or two of my favorite essential oil onto my light bulb and inside my dresser drawers.
- After a hard workout, I like to mist my face with a cool spray of water and eucalyptus oil. Put these two ingredients into a clean spray bottle, shake, close your eyes, and give yourself a refreshing spritz.
- When I'm meditating, I enjoy burning incense. It is not only delicious to smell, it also has a highly spiritual quality to it. In fact, it has been used in the spiritual purification rituals of many cultures, from American Indian sweat lodges to Muslim mosques.

Other ideas:

- Essential oils are great for giving or receiving a massage.
- Burn candles in your favorite scents.
- Some scents can be sprinkled on your carpet and then vacuumed up. The aroma will hang in your room for days.
- Occasionally open your window and let in the smells of outside. Try to identify as many of the scents as you can.
- Drink herbal tea. Not only does the tea itself calm or energize, the aroma of the tea works its own magic.
- Bath time is the perfect chance to try out scented soaps and bubble baths.

Don't Forget Essential Oils

What exactly are essential oils? These strong-scented substances are distilled from plants (bark, seeds, flowers, etc.), and can usually be found in health food stores or beauty supply shops. They are concentrated, so a very small amount of oil is all it takes to produce a large effect. Essential oils can be a fun part of aromatherapy. Most can be applied directly to the skin, or you can diffuse them by mixing with vegetable oil or dropping into bath water.

So that's the scoop on aromatherapy. However, the art of sensual smelling isn't limited to the above. You can enjoy scents in millions of ways. "Stop and smell the roses," is excellent advice. Pay attention to the smells of your life: flowers, shampoo, grass, and cookies. These simple observations will rejuvenate your spirits. The smells you love most are a part of who you are. Pay attention to the messages they are sending you!

YOUR ROOM TO DREAM

Now that you have analyzed the objects in your room and how they make you feel, you may want to take a few minutes and write in a notebook or journal. What objects reflect you best? What colors are you most drawn to? How do they make you feel? Have you learned anything new about yourself from the aromas and objects you love the most? As you grow and change, your taste will too. Pay attention to the messages that your space sends you, and use these ideas to create places that are sacred all around you! Your sacred space may change and develop over time, but it should always reflect who you are, your thoughts and dreams, and your own soul searching.

RESOURCES

Altars: Bringing Sacred Shrines into Your Everyday Life, by Denise Linn

The Art of Aromatherapy: A Guide to Using Essential Oils for Health and Relaxation, by Pamela Allardice

Clear Your Clutter with Feng Shui, by Karen Kingston

Color Style: How to Identify the Colors That Are Right For Your Home, by Carolyn Warrender

Move Your Stuff, Change Your Life: How to Use Feng Shui to Get Love, Money, Respect, and Happiness, by Karen Rauch Carter

101 Feng Shui Tips for the Home, by Richard Webster

500 Formulas for Aromatherapy: Mixing Essential Oils for Every Use, by David and Carol Schiller

The Illustrated Encyclopedia of Feng Shui: The Complete Guide to the Art and Practice of Feng Shui, by Lillian Too

CHAPTER 3

Set Your Body Free

YOGA, MASSAGE, AND THE SPA TREATMENT

Our bodies: we can't escape them. We see them every day, rain or shine, like it or not. We're often taught to hate our bodies, and it's been said that almost eighty percent of girls do. We punish them, starve them, stuff them, and hide them. If only we could learn to work *with* our bodies instead of against them, we'd be much happier people.

Even though soul searching may seem like a mostly mental and emotional journey, the mind, body, and spirit are closely linked. When we have negative feelings about our physical selves, it makes it almost impossible to focus on our emotional and spiritual identities. How can we expect to understand and accept something we hate looking at in the mirror?

For many of us, the biggest hurdle in soul searching is learning to toss aside society's physical expectations. All too often, we replace our quest for wisdom and self-understanding with the pursuit of other ideals: thinness, sexiness, beauty. To cope with these pressures, we've got to strengthen the union between the body and the mind. There are many tools that can help us, from dance to yoga to exercise. When we honor the body's needs for movement, nourishment, and relaxation, we send ourselves a message that these needs are important. When we fulfill these needs, we become more in tune with them. Listening to our bodies is perfect training for learning to understand and meet the needs of our soul as well.

Becoming comfortable with ourselves takes time. It also takes guts. The reason feeling satisfied with ourselves can be risky business is that so many people out there are secretly against it. It's what we call a "double standard": we're told to love our bodies, but we risk punishment if we do. Many people are threatened by female security, often because it invokes their own fear and jealousy. For example, I once had to wear a leotard for a school performance. As I was waiting backstage, dancing around crazily and joking with my friends, I heard a classmate whisper to his friend, "Who does she think she is? It's not like she has anything to be proud of!" The leotard that made me feel fabulous and elegant a few seconds before now painfully screamed the fact that my breasts were too small and my thighs too muscular. I ran to the locker room and put a sweatshirt over my outfit. Looking back on this experience, I wish I had gathered enough courage to march up to that boy, give him a piece of my mind, and go back to dancing in my leotard.

Think about your past. You've probably received similar messages about your body. You may feel as though you should parade it if you want to be popular and get attention, but at the same time you know you might feel you should hide it unless you want to be ridiculed. Are you comfortable with who you are and the way you look? If not, don't stress. It takes time. You have to learn about your body and understand it, inside and out. As you do, you will be amazed at the way your physical well-being affects your emotional and spiritual health as well. This chapter is full of fun ideas to help you nurture, strengthen, and honor your body.

BODY CELEBRATION

There are probably objects all around you that you have memorized— the scribblings on the cover of a notebook, the way your cat's hair grows, or the freckles on your best friend's face. When we observe something daily, we start to memorize size, color, and texture. But how well do we know our own bodies? Take a minute to think about it. Do you understand your physiology and how the various systems of your body function? If not, read up on your anatomy and pay attention during science class! The human body is an absolutely amazing, beautiful thing. After learning the basics from textbooks and teachers, you are responsible for learning about your own individual body.

Spend some time getting to know your body. What are your toes shaped like? How about your ears? What birthmarks, scars, freckles, and moles do you have? While you may feel strange having to learn about your own body, these are discoveries you ought to make. Try standing in front of the mirror. View yourself objectively. Tell yourself everything you love about your body. When you are done, thank your body for the many gifts it offers up every day. Think about all it gives you, including the ability to run, eat, heal wounds, and see the world. These are incredible blessings, and you owe it a lot! When you feel you really know your body, you can decide whether or not you have the guts to say: "This is me. I accept who I am and what I look like."

EXERCISE

Believe it or not, exercise can be a great tool for self-discovery. When you play sports, you make both

What do YOU think?

For the most part, there is not one part of my body that I really want to change. I'm happy with the way it is right now. For me, I think I'm the way I'm supposed to look.
—RACHAEL BENTSEN, AGE 15

I feel nowhere near as comfortable about my body as I did just a few years ago. The stereotype of "stick-thin equals beautiful" is still strong. One of my friends and I were talking about this. We looked at ourselves in the mirror and said, "You know . . . I think society is getting to us." I feel that every person should feel good about themselves, but part of the solution for this would be to wipe out stereotypes.
—ANONYMOUS

My body is the greatest instrument I could ever own. I use it at every opportunity I get, even when it's just dancing in my bedroom when my favorite song comes on the radio. It's such a wonderful gift, why waste it?
—EMMARIE HUETTEMAN, AGE 13

body and soul feel confident and strong by focusing your mind on what your body can do. Did you know that girls who exercise are more likely to get good grades, feel happier, and be more confident? They are also less likely to get involved in drugs, become pregnant during teenage years, and struggle with depression. Exercising regularly will help you release stress, focus your mind, increase your energy, and nourish your spirit. If you're feeling frustrated or angry, a good workout may help you feel better, because exercise produces *endorphins*. These chemicals in the human body give us a sense of happiness, peace, and exhilaration. Exercise is basically a natural high! So find something fun—biking, roller-blading, hiking, snowboarding, dancing, fencing—and make your body and soul feel better. Exercising for just 30 minutes, three times a week, should do the trick.

YOGA

What is yoga? You've probably heard of it or seen it on TV. Although it's a relatively new trend in America, people have been practicing yoga in the East for thousands of years. Yoga is a combination of meditation and exercise that is done through various stretching poses. The word "yoga" means union of body and mind. Yoga can help you learn to focus your mind sharply on your body's needs and feelings.

Although yoga is relatively simple to do, the benefits are amazing. It calms your mind, tones your muscles, increases flexibility, and improves the alignment of your body so that energy can flow freely. Yoga gurus know that when we are feeling mental or spiritual stress, it is reflected in our bodies. To prove this to yourself, just think of how tight your shoulders become when you are cramming for a big test! Yoga poses help us increase our control over our bodies while releasing the tension in our muscles. You will be amazed at how this releases mental stress at the same time!

Starting Out

Are you ready? Let's get going! Some of the basic yoga moves can be learned at home without much trouble. Yoga requires few supplies and can benefit everyone, regardless of how flexible. A soft yoga mat or towel, loose clothing, and calming music can all be helpful. Also, your muscles loosen up better if the room is warm.

As you do these poses, it is very important to listen to your body and be careful with yourself. In gym or ballet, you might have stretched your muscles as far as they could possibly go. But in yoga, the emphasis is not on stretching the farthest. It is much more important that you keep your body in the correct posture and alignment. Be patient and gentle with yourself! Don't ever push your muscles to the point of pain. Instead, focus on keeping your back straight, your shoulders relaxed, and your joints open and aligned. Listen to your own body and don't compare yourself to anyone else.

Beginning the Poses

Hatha yoga, the yoga of the body, involves warming up for a few minutes of relaxation in the *Corpse Pose*, before moving on to other poses, called *asanas*. **Corpse Pose.** You may have already guessed how to do this pose, just by the name. Lie flat on your back, arms out at your sides with palms facing up. Breathe deeply (as described in Chapter 4) and relax. Stretch out your spine as though someone were pulling your head away from your feet. Imagine your weight sinking deeper and deeper into the floor. Focus on relaxing each part of your body, starting at your feet and moving up toward your head. When you reach your face, focus on relaxing your throat, cheeks, eyes, and scalp in turn. As you enter deep relaxation, feel your mind growing clear and calm. When you have spent about five minutes in the Corpse Pose, you will be ready to begin other poses. I like to start by gently shrugging my shoulders, circling my neck, and flexing my legs. Here are three beginning poses to try:

Cat Pose (**Vidalasana**). This pose is known for aiding digestion and relieving stomach and menstrual cramps. Begin by kneeling on all fours. Your knees and hands should be shoulder width apart, with your arms and thighs perpendicular to the floor. Look up towards the wall. Inhale by making a hissing sound

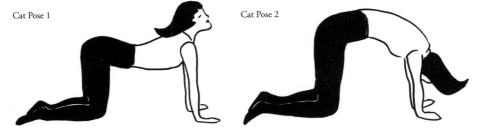

Cat Pose 1

Cat Pose 2

with your mouth. Then arch your back like a cat while lowering your head. Hold the pose and your breath for a few moments, then return to your original position. Repeat this pose three times.

Triangle Pose (**Trikonasana**). The triangle pose is great for improving circulation and muscle tone. In a standing position, spread your legs about three feet apart. Feet should point straight ahead of you. Bend at the waist and twist to the left as you stretch your right-hand fingers to touch your right toe and your left hand reaches for the sky. Make sure to keep your knees straight during this pose. If your hamstrings are tight, put a book next to your foot, and rest your hand there instead of on the floor. As

Triangle Pose

you relax into the pose, slowly turn your neck to look up at your left hand and hold for a few moments. Slowly return to your original standing position. Repeat this pose three times for each side of the body.

Downward Facing Dog Pose (**Uttanasana**). You can use the dog pose to relieve nervousness, anxiety, and depression. Begin in a standing position, feet together. As you exhale a breath, bend forward and place the palms of your hands on

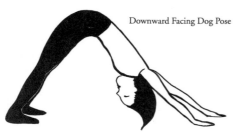

Downward Facing Dog Pose

the floor (or as low as feels comfortable) and as close to your feet as you can. Lift your head to look ahead of you and take several breaths. Then exhale and gently move your upper body closer to your legs until you feel a nice stretch in your hamstrings. Breathe. Hold this position for several moments. Then lift your head again and take two deep breaths. Slowly return to a standing position.

When you are done with the poses you wish to do, end your practice by re-entering the Corpse Pose.

Finding a Class

These poses should get you started. If you like them, there are hundreds of other yoga poses you can learn through books, videos, and classes (see the resources below and at the end of this chapter). It is probably best to attend a class if you are really serious about practicing yoga. A good instructor and a safe, nurturing environment can help you reach the full benefits of yoga. If there is a teen yoga class near you, I would definitely recommend it, because learning yoga with your peers (especially other girls) can be an amazing experience. You can find yoga classes through the phone book, health food stores, fitness centers, community colleges, word of mouth, or contact these organizations for yoga classes in your area:

United States Yoga Association
2159 Filbert Street
San Francisco, California 94123
Phone: (415) 931-YOGA
Web: *www.usyoga.org*

The American Yoga Association
P.O. Box 19986
Sarasota, Florida 34276
Phone: (941) 927-4977
Web: *americanyogaassociation.org*

MASSAGE

Massage is another wonderful way to heal and celebrate your body. The act of massaging muscles helps to increase circulation, stretch ligaments and tendons, cleanse toxins, and relieve pain—not to mention relax you! But have you realized that massage can also affect your emotions? Spiritually, during a massage, we feel an intense communication of compassion and positive energy.

Although professional massages can cost a lot of money, you can do it at home for free! I am sure that you know the basics of massage. Here are a few pointers to help you whether you are massaging yourself or treating a friend.

1. Many people around the world believe that massaging the feet and hands will actually benefit the whole body. Hand and foot massages are probably the easiest types of massage to give yourself. Before you start, soak your feet in warm water.

2. Always massage toward the heart. By massaging toward the heart, you can improve your body's blood circulation and relax your muscles.

3. Use aromatherapy. Scented oils and incenses can help you and your muscles relax deeply.

4. Try slightly warming up some scented massage oil in the microwave. This will also help your fingers move easily over the skin.

5. Try different motions with your hands. Make gentle circles. Use your knuckles. Try tapping lightly with the sides of your hands.

6. As you push up with the balls of your hands, clench the loose skin gently with your fingers. Pretend that you are kneading pizza dough! Get creative and discover what feels best to you.

Reflexology

For over 5,000 years, people have used reflexology to stimulate overall body health and release tension. There are even paintings of the ancient Egyptians practicing reflexology to cure illness. Reflexology is the belief that certain areas of your feet correspond to different parts of your body, and that by massaging those areas of the feet, you can stimulate or heal the related parts of the body.

But you don't have to be an ancient Chinese master to benefit from foot massage. If you have a big test coming up, gently pinch your toes to stimulate your brain. If you're feeling queasy, try massaging the arch of your left foot to relieve the

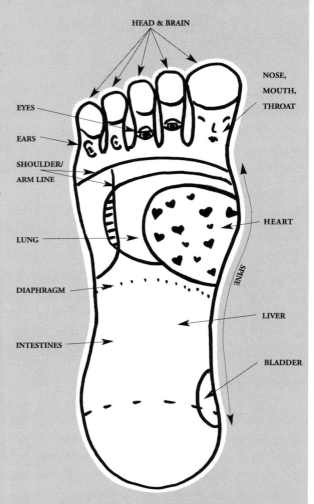

HEAD & BRAIN

NOSE, MOUTH, THROAT

EYES

EARS

SHOULDER/ARM LINE

HEART

LUNG

SPINE

DIAPHRAGM

LIVER

INTESTINES

BLADDER

Reflexology

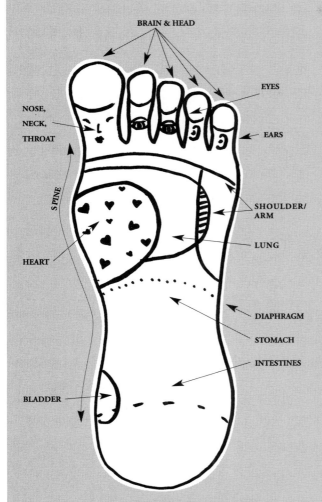

BRAIN & HEAD

EYES

NOSE,
NECK,
THROAT

EARS

SPINE

SHOULDER/
ARM

LUNG

HEART

DIAPHRAGM

STOMACH

INTESTINES

BLADDER

stomachache. Offer your mom a foot massage after a long day at work or experiment on your friends to see which pressure points work best. (Beware, this may be challenging for people who are particularly ticklish!)

Begin by moving your thumb and fingers softly along the sides of each foot. Then stimulate the different pressure points with a firm and gentle massage. Follow the reflexology chart and work your way through all the different regions of the foot, starting with the head (toes) and working your way down to the intestines (heel), until you've covered pressure points for the entire body. Gently squeeze each foot when you're finished.

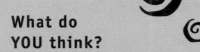

What do YOU think?

YOU DESERVE THE SPA TREATMENT

Suppose you've tried yoga, you've tried the foot massage, and yet you're still nervous about that upcoming final. Your neck is in knots and you're exhausted from all the studying. It's obviously time to pamper your body! You don't need to go to a real spa in order to hold a day of healing. The following spa activities are fun and relaxing, but they also send an important message to your body and soul. They say that you care about your needs and you want to fulfill them. The spa treatment gives you quiet time to relax, step away from life, and focus on what you and your body are really feeling. As you do these activities, you may also want to try some breathing or meditation exercises (see the next chapter). Listen to your body and do whatever it takes to relax and clear your mind.

Starting Your Retreat

To begin a spa treatment, find a quiet time in the day when you won't be bothered. Let your family know that you'd like some time to yourself when they won't interrupt you. Place all reminders of reality out of sight—your homework, your calendar, your phone, and your list of errands. Put a kettle of water on the stove and make yourself some tea. Now, let the good times roll!

Beautiful Baths

There are tons of fun things you can do to melt away stress. I happen to think the best way to start is with a warm bath. When I was little, I spent hours in the tub, playing with plastic toys and soap suds. I had so much fun! Then I moved on to taking showers because they were faster, and the magical world of the bath became a distant memory. Recently, I have rediscovered this sacred pleasure.

I've been concocting special bath recipes that change my tub from a childhood playpen into an elegant relaxation haven. Here are some bath recipes you can use to kick off your relaxation-fest:

The Out-At-Sea Bath. *This exfoliating bath leaves you with soft, lovely skin, and brings the regenerative properties of the ocean right to your own bathroom.*

As you fill the bathtub with comfortably warm (not hot) water, slowly add a cup full of sea salts (you can find these at an aromatherapy store or even a pharmacy). Save a bit of the salt, and use it to rub over your body before entering the bath. After soaking for about ten minutes, take a body brush or loofah and stroke your skin in an upward motion, brushing toward your head. When you're ready to get out, take a quick rinse in a cool shower. This is one of the most invigorating and energizing experiences you'll ever have!

The Romantic's Bath. *This bath not only leaves your skin more supple and smooth, but it will leave you feeling dreamy and creative!*

Pour in some coconut oil under the heat of your running bath water, adding a few drops of your favorite essential oil (also available at aromatherapy stores). Rose, sandalwood, or rosemary work particularly well, and can be purchased at most health food stores. Sprinkle some rose petals into the water and soak, pretending you are a spoiled princess!

The Sweet Dreams Bath. *This one is best to do in the evening, after a tough day. It is supposed to bring you relaxation and peaceful dreams.*

While preparing a warm bath, toss in three chamomile tea bags and ten drops of lavender essential oil. After the tea bags have steeped in the bath water, enter the bath and remove the tea bags, placing them on your closed eyelids. Position some scented candles or incense nearby and breathe deeply, letting any tension in your body dissolve.

Fabulous Facials

The muscles on your face do a lot of work during the day! They help you express all your words and emotions, but get very little thanks in return. Pampering your face is a great way to thank your body. Although you could waste your money on expensive facials or skin creams, there are plenty of natural remedies you can make at home without much hassle. Did you know that honey

What would YOU do for a Spa Party?

My friends and I would light aromatherapy candles, put cucumbers on our eyes, and play outside in the rain.

—ALYSSA LOTT, AGE 13

If any time of year merits a "Spa Party," final exam time would be it. I'd invite my friends over for a "study session," but make sure they wore their pajamas so they could "concentrate better." Once they arrived, I'd lock their books in a closet and give them books from the 70s on homemade beauty recipes. There would be two rules at the party: all attendees must be relaxed at all times, and they may not worry about anything other than what goes into the banana face cream.

—EMMARIE HUETTEMAN, AGE 13

We'd give and receive massages, paint our nails, do face masks, read inspirational and interesting passages from our favorite authors, and do yoga.

—MOLLY BRANNAN, AGE 16

is a great moisturizer? Were you aware that oatmeal is the perfect exfoliator, and lemon juice is a safe, natural hair lightener? It's about time you learned some of history's oldest spa secrets. The following recipes will get you started:

Steamy Herbal Facial

You'll Need:
- ⊚ Boiling water
- ⊚ Large bowl
- ⊚ Dried herbs (rosemary, thyme, or even flower petals)
- ⊚ A clean towel

Here's How: Put a tea kettle of water on the stove to boil. When the water is ready, carefully pour the hot water into a bowl on your counter. Now add a handful of dried herbs or flowers. Make sure your hair is out of your face, and put a towel over your head. Lower your face carefully towards the water. Don't get too close, of course, and test the steam's heat with your hand first! Use the towel as if it were a tent trapping the steam between you and the bowl. Close your eyes and let your head hover over the basin of fragrant, steaming water for five to ten minutes. Your pores will slowly open up and begin to sweat a little, as if you were in a sauna. Enjoy the heat and calming scents. When you are done, rinse your face with a gentle cleanser and splash with cool water to re-close your pores. Moisturize and enjoy the clean, fresh feeling of your skin.

Super-Sweet Face Mask

You'll Need:
- 2 tablespoons honey
- 1 egg yolk
- warm wash cloth

Here's How: Didn't I tell you that honey is a great natural moisturizer? It makes a great face mask for dry skin, especially when combined with an egg yolk. Mix these ingredients together in a bowl, apply mixture to your face (avoiding the eye area) and let it sit for five to ten minutes. Then gently rinse away with a warm wash cloth. Voilà—soft, smooth, honey-smelling skin!

Grapefruit and Oatmeal Scrub

You'll Need:
- 1 tablespoon pure grapefruit juice
- 3-4 tablespoons plain oatmeal
- warm wash cloth

Here's How: Mix the grapefruit juice and oatmeal into a fine paste. Smooth it over your face, leaving it there for fifteen minutes. When the time is up, use your warm washcloth or your wet fingertips to massage the scrub over your face. Rinse off with cool water. This face mask is a great cleansing scrub for normal to oily skin.

LISTEN TO YOUR BODY

There are so many fun ways to honor your body, I can't possibly cover them all in one chapter. Get creative when it comes to self-indulgence. Turn on beautiful music and dance. Make a steam room for yourself by closing the door to the bathroom and running a hot shower. Give yourself a pedicure. Do any exercise that feels good! During a stressful time, have a spa party and invite all your friends to relax together and help pamper each other. Use massage and yoga to help you, or ask friends to share their best relaxation tips. As feminist Gloria Steinem once wrote, "If we bless our bodies, they will bless us." Listening to your body and learning to honor and love it is a crucial part of soul searching.

RESOURCES

Everything You Need to Know About Yoga: An Introduction for Teens, by Stefanie Weiss

Natural Home Spa, by Sian Rees

Living Yoga: A.M./P.M. Yoga for Beginners Set, Living Yoga (Primary Contributor), et al, videotape

Throw Like a Girl: Discovering the Body, Mind, and Spirit of the Athlete in You!, by Shelley Frost and Ann Troussieux

Water Magic: Healing Bath Recipes for the Body, Spirit, and Soul, by Mary Muryn

When Women Stop Hating Their Bodies: Freeing Yourself from Food and Weight Obsession, by Jane R. Hirschmann and Carol H. Munter

Yoga for Teens: How to Improve Your Fitness, Confidence, Appearance, and Health—And Have Fun Doing It!, by Thia Luby

CHAPTER 4

Focus Your Mind

RELAXATION, MEDITATION, AND VISUALIZATION

An alarm clock shrieks in your ear. You jump out of bed, remembering the homework you didn't finish. You take a quick shower, get dressed, and rush to school with a Pop-Tart still warm in your hand. When the last bell rings, after seven long hours of tests and lectures, your gym bag is already in your hand and you shuffle through the crowded halls toward soccer practice. After soccer comes your flute lesson, dinner, homework, and bed. If you're lucky, you'll be able to fall asleep despite the tornado of thoughts whirling in your head: *Why didn't he call me? I hope we win the game tomorrow! Is Sandra mad at me?*

This kind of frantic day isn't unusual for the average teenager. We have so much to worry about: school, sex, sports, friends. Our minds are so full of emotions and desires that we hardly have time to sort them out. All of this stress can take its toll on our bodies and intellect, which is why relaxation techniques are so important. They help us convert **negative** stress into **healthy** stress.

Healthy stress? Yes, stress can be good for us when it comes in the right amounts. It adds a dash of excitement to our life, like the boost some people get from singing before an audience or playing in a championship basketball game. Yet too much stress leaves us overwhelmed, anxious, and unhappy.

THE POWER OF QUIET

What's the point of living in a draining stress whirlwind when we can have peace of mind instead? Physically, relaxation is better for our hearts, blood pressure,

Quiz: Test Your Stress

1. I consider my stress level to be:
    a) Relatively low. I have a lot to do, but I know how to prioritize my time.
    b) It depends. Sometimes I feel super-stressed, other times I'm cool as a cucumber.
    c) AHHHHH! I'm too stressed to talk about stress!

2. How often do you spend time doing what you love, like reading or painting?
    a) Only on weekends.
    b) I try to do something I love every day. Even on hurried days, I find a bit of time for myself.
    c) Yeah, right! I hardly have time to brush my teeth.

3. When a minor annoyance occurs, such as spilling milk on your math home-work or getting a big zit on the day of school pictures, how do you react?
    a) I can't stand how unfair life is. Bad things always seem to happen to me.
    b) I remind myself, "Hey, it could be worse!"
    c) I think about how much the situation sucks, and then I remind myself, "Hey, it could be worse!"

4. When I've had a stressful week, I usually:
    a) Relax by watching TV or playing Nintendo while eating ice cream.
    b) Hide out in my room, cry, and start dreading the week to come.
    c) Take a warm bath, write in my journal, and think about how I can make next week better.

5. Lately, I think my life is:
    a) Satisfying. I'm thankful for everything I have, even though things aren't always easy.
    b) Tiring. Sometimes I'm too exhausted and stressed to realize all of the wonderful things I've got going for me.
    c) A roller-coaster. I have my great days, and I have my horrible ones.

Score Your Answers:

1. a) 3   b) 2   c) 1
2. a) 2   b) 3   c) 1
3. a) 1   b) 3   c) 2
4. a) 2   b) 1   c) 3
5. a) 3   b) 1   c) 2

15-12 points: Wow! You are a stress-handling diva!

You understand that anxiety is a natural part of life, and you've learned how to deal accordingly. Take yourself to the next level by mastering some challenging relaxation techniques, such as yoga and meditation.

11-7 points: You're on the right track.

Sometimes your life is great, other times it's not so hot. If you start using some basic relaxation techniques, such as visualization, your stress-level will dissipate and you'll notice the great times beginning to outnumber the "not so hot" ones.

6 or less points: Learn how to chill out.

During stressful moments, try to step outside the problem and ask yourself, "Will this matter to me one year from now?" Misplacing your favorite bracelet may seem like a cataclysmic event at the time, but it won't affect you in the long run. You may think that you don't have time to relax, but you really owe it to yourself to try. Even just a few minutes of deep breathing exercises can make a big difference.

What do YOU think?

Being a teenager stresses me out. When kids are seven or eight they dream of being a teenager. Now that I'm in the middle of those years, I can tell you that all of my friends and I are ready for our teens to be over. You're caught in the middle. You don't feel quite right playing with dolls, but you know that you really aren't ready for serious dating. You can't be ten, and you can't be twenty. You have to be somewhere in the middle. It's frustrating and annoying, and sometimes depressing. I think that's why so many teens feel lost and don't know where their lives are going.

—GILLIAN McHALE, AGE 15

and energy levels. Mentally, through practices such as meditation and yoga, relaxation has even more to offer: better concentration, alleviation of depression, and a greater flow of creativity.

Meditation in particular is a powerful vehicle of self-discovery. To meditate means to observe our minds in action. When you taste a really rich piece of chocolate or receive a fantastic massage from a friend, do you ever close your eyes and savor the sensation? Meditating is much like this act of focus and intensification. By closing our eyes, silencing distractions, and really listening to our minds and hearts, we can feel more intensely who we really are. We begin to shed our outer shells, and our innermost selves unfold. This union between mind and soul brings us to our core—a place where we often have no words to fall back on, only sensations.

In this chapter, we will learn several meditation techniques. Meditation is a form of relaxation in which you train your mind to focus on absolutely *nothing*. This is much more difficult than it may sound. However, as author Maureen Garth reminds us, "[Meditation] is not beyond the reach of anyone, provided they take the time and create the opportunity." To meditate, you need nothing but a quiet spot and your own willing mind.

BREATHING

Learning how to breathe correctly is vital to the proper practice of meditation, visualization, and yoga. "I've known how to breathe since the moment I was born," you might be thinking. "If I didn't know how to do it correctly, I'd be dead!" This isn't necessarily true. Obviously you have the ability to breathe, but you probably don't do it as well as you should. Most people use only twenty percent of their lungs' total capacity each time they take a breath. Their bodies could be receiving double this amount of oxygen if they learned how to breathe correctly. And extra oxygen is amazingly beneficial! It can improve skin tone, reduce stress, increase muscle performance, and help you think more clearly.

Take a minute to listen to your breathing. Is it shallow or deep? Which part of your chest is it filling? Ideally, you should inhale from your nose, pushing your diaphragm down and expanding your abdomen. Your breath should fill your chest cavity from the bottom to the top, without raising your shoulders. As you exhale, slowly release as much air as possible from your lungs. The exhalation is very important, since it removes stale air to make room for a fresh inhalation. Try this style of breathing for ten slow breaths. How did that make you feel? More relaxed?

Use these deep breathing exercises as you prepare yourself for deeper meditations. You can also use deep breathing during any moment when you need to relax or clear your mind. Whether it is before a big game or in the morning when you're still in bed, those ten deep breaths can give you an amazing burst of energy and clarity, while also calming you.

MEDITATION

Although there are many different types of meditation, all of them involve clearing the mind and relaxing. *This can be surprisingly difficult.* It takes a great amount of discipline to quiet the voices constantly competing for attention inside our heads. The goal of meditation is to get as close as possible to silence, even if our thoughts intrude every once in a while. No matter how hard we try, these thoughts can be almost impossible to hush completely at first. But with daily practice it gets easier. You can do meditation almost anywhere—use it to gain a little inner peace before diving into that math test!

How to Meditate

1. To begin, find a peaceful place where you will not be disturbed. Lay comfortably on the ground or sit cross-legged with a pillow or blanket elevating your pelvic bone. Close your eyes and breathe out of your nose only. Don't consciously alter the rhythm of your breathing—just listen to it.

2. After about five minutes of listening to your breath, begin to take control of your inhalations by making them fuller and deeper as you learned in the section above. Imagine that your abdomen is a balloon you are filling and releasing.

3. Try to keep your mind clear. Think "calm" on your inhale and "relaxed" on your exhale. Focus on just these two words and the air coming in and going out of your nose. Think of nothing else but these words. Whenever a thought or worry comes into your head, pretend it is a soap bubble. Let it pop or float away, whichever you prefer.

4. If a particular thought continues to bother you, take a second to write it down on a piece of paper before continuing your meditation. Writing in your journal before meditation can be a good way to organize your thoughts and prepare your mind.

5. Continue meditating for as long as you feel comfortable. When you are finished meditating, don't just jump up and race off to your next task. Move slowly as you bring your awareness back to the room around you.

Tame Your Monkey Mind

Virtually all beginning meditators find the task of quieting their minds overwhelming and frustrating. The brain has a natural tendency to babble, rushing at lightning speed from thought to thought. Buddhists call this the "Monkey Mind," and it is the number one reason why many new meditation students quit before discovering the true benefits of sitting still. If you think of your mind as a monkey in the jungle, constantly swinging from branch to branch, taking few pauses in between, you can view your journey into meditation as a quest to "tame the monkey."

In the beginning, concentrate on taming your monkey mind for just five minutes at a time. Don't be frustrated; it gets easier with practice. Focus on your breathing when your concentration escapes you. As you get better at clearing your mind, expand the length of your meditation sessions. Half-hour sessions are ideal, but any amount of time is worth it. Try to spend at least ten minutes meditating every day. On really busy days when you don't have time for

Special Meditations

Tonal Meditation:

Some people like to add a word or sound to their meditation to help them focus. Try chanting a word (silently or aloud), such as love, God, mother, calm, relax, or peace, each time you inhale and exhale.

Color Meditation:

Choose a color that you associate with a certain benefit, such as pink for love or yellow for energy. Allow this color to wash over you and fill you as you meditate. When you inhale, imagine that you are breathing in this color. When you exhale, imaging you are breathing out the impurities within you.

Ohhmm...

Water Meditation:

Fill a clear glass with water and hold it between your hands. Don't let your hands touch each other. Then, for at least five minutes, look down into the glass and observe. You may see colors, swirls of energy, or just plain old water. Keep your focus on the water until the time is up, then drink it. Many people believe that your energy and concentration will turn the water into a special "tonic," supplying your body with whatever it needs at the time.

Problem Meditation:

If you have a problem or a question, think about it before meditating and then let your subconscious work on it during the meditation. Don't try to think about your problem or question during the meditation. Just pay attention to what thoughts or images pop into your mind. These may be the keys to the solution or the answer for you. Listen to your inner wisdom. This is the heart of soul searching.

a long meditation, use the spare time in the car or in the shower to do your deep breathing and clear your mind. Even one minute of meditation will make you feel calmer and more centered. Meditation is something that you can do anywhere, anytime.

As you become better at it, you will begin to feel the benefits. It will help you handle stress better and relax more easily. If you have a difficult time falling asleep, a breathing meditation is much better than counting sheep!

VISUALIZATION

A full moon. An erupting volcano. A bowl of ripe strawberries. Do these words bring certain distinct images into your mind? The art of mentally picturing these words is called visualization. Visualization is a type of meditation that requires us to focus our minds on an image in order to create a particular feeling: peace, energy, confidence, or whatever else we might desire. By taking us on simulated adventures, our brains are forced to burst through reality's barriers and enter the realm of the imagination.

Keep in mind that we don't need a perfectly crisp image in our heads in order to visualize it. In fact, most people don't see clear-cut pictures. I tend to see murky outlines, and I've met plenty of people who say they sense, feel, or even smell an image instead of getting a visual picture. With experience, the clarity of your visualizations will improve, so be patient.

I always keep a journal nearby when I do visualization exercises, just in case I have an insight worthy of recording. Before beginning, I like to do some simple breathing warm-ups to clear my mind. In a comfortable place where I know I won't be disturbed, I sit back or lie down on the floor. After observing the patterns of my breath for a moment, I make each inhalation deeper and each exhalation slower. Focusing on the breath and deepening it is a great preparation for all types of meditating.

Getting Started

Any scenery that you find relaxing or meaningful is a good starting point for a visualization. Tropical beaches, snow-covered mountainsides, and lush forests are popular places to visualize, or you can invent your own magical land transcendent of all reality. Regardless of what you're visualizing, don't just see it— experience it. Involve your mind intensely in the details of the scene: the sound of water trickling over rocks, the scent of lavender buds, the touch of cool mist against your cheek. Discover how real the situation can become.

If you're trying visualization for the first time, you may find it helpful to follow a written meditation. If you have trouble memorizing it, tape record it or have a friend read it out loud to you. Here are two visualizations to try:

1. Beach Adventure

Warm up with some deep breathing, close your eyes, and relax. You are on a spectacular island beach. Amazed at the sapphire clarity of the water and the softness of the white, powdery sand, you spend a moment taking in the scene. Although the sun is gently warming your face, the fresh, salty breeze keeps you cool. The sky is a vast expanse of blue, speckled with a few white puffs of clouds. You begin to walk toward the water, digging your toes into the soft, warm sand. You are totally relaxed and carefree.

When you reach the water's edge, you let the foam of the waves tickle your toes. You stand in peace, gazing at the horizon. You hear a joyful squeak and see a dolphin approaching. He is calling for you to play with him. So you splash into the cool, sparkling water.

Wrapping your arms around the dolphin's strong, rubbery back, you let him carry you out to sea. Starting slowly, and gradually gaining speed, the dolphin takes you soaring across the surface of the ocean. Your hair whips in the wind and the water sprays your face. You feel exhilarated, fearless, and free.

After a thrilling ride, the dolphin carries you back to shore. At the water's edge again, you thank him and give him a slippery hug goodbye. You walk back to the soft white sand and dry off under the summer sun, taking in the sweet scent of the flowers growing all around you. You feel blessed to bask in the sun's energizing rays. As you listen to the lapping waves, you are intensely calm, loving, and in sync with the rhythms of the Earth.

You know it is time to return home. You take one last look at the clear sea and begin your journey home. Counting slowly to five, you prepare to open your eyes. Five . . . four . . . three . . . breathe deeply . . . two . . . one . . . you can open your eyes and stretch. You are home.

2. Forest Reverie

Warm up with some deep breathing, close your eyes and relax. You're in the mountains. The air is crisp and filled with the fresh scent of pine and cedar. As you walk on the soft forest floor, you feel the gentle crush of pine needles beneath your feet. Somewhere in the distance you can hear the soft gurgle of a mountain stream. Following the sound, you discover a creek winding its way through green ferns and purple wildflowers.

The creek is crystal clear and near the edges of the stream bed beautiful moss and lichen are growing. The water sliding over the stones in the stream has made each stone perfectly round. You kneel at the water's edge and pick up a dark stone, cool and wet from the water, and hold it in the center of your palm. The weight of the stone brings to mind security, strength, and calmness. Searching the horizon, you can see in the distance the sun shining through a small clearing in the forest.

You gently replace the stone and rise, walking toward the clearing. As you enter the forest, you notice a deer nibbling on some green leaves. The deer looks up at you with her large brown eyes, then turns. Somehow you know that you should follow her. The doe leads you through the clearing and under a cluster of giant cedars. You hear the rushing of water and arrive at a great, shimmering waterfall. Mist rises all around you as white veils of water fall from overhanging rocks into a deep green pool. Delicate moss and ferns, covered with jeweled water drops, surround the waterfall,

You step into the shallow pool and walk toward the falls. The mist rises all around you as you let the cool and refreshing waterfall spray on your face. It trickles through your hair, over your shoulders, and down your back. You stand completely under the falls and let the water flow over your whole body. You feel your worries and anxieties carried away by the rushing water, into the deep green pool, and away down the stream. After several moments, you step out, invigorated and relaxed.

You know it is time to return home. You take one last look at the waterfall and begin your journey home. Counting slowly to five, you prepare to open your eyes. Five . . . four . . . three . . . breathe deeply . . . two . . . one . . . you can open your eyes and stretch. You are home.

RELAXING YOUR WAY

It is easy to let the stress of everyday life overwhelm and confuse us. But if we take the time to step back from our lives and silence our minds, we can find a peaceful place to explore our souls. The techniques of meditation, visualization, and deep breathing have incredible power when we make room for them in our lives. Sometimes we are so busy, we don't even have time to fully understand our own emotions. How can we hope to resolve our problems if we don't fully know them first? I hope that you will take the time to seek out the quiet in your life. Within that space, you can begin the journey to understand the complex and beautiful person you are!

RESOURCES

The Art of Awakening Spirit, by Carol Kurtz Walsh

Creative Visualization Meditations, by Shakti Gawain (audiocassette)

101 Essential Tips: Basic Meditation, by Naomi Ozaniec and Deni Bown

Wherever You Go There You Are: Mindfulness Meditation in Everyday Life, by Jon Kabat-Zinn

CHAPTER 5

Find the Key to Your Soul

KEEPING A JOURNAL

On the first day of second grade, my teacher, Ms. Llanes, walked down the rows of desks, handing out black and white speckled notebooks. "These journals will become your best friends," she told us. "You will write in them every day, no matter how little or how much you have to tell them." I nodded my head excitedly and squeezed my journal tightly to my chest. I was already thinking what to name it. Melanie? Patty? In the end, I decided to call my journal "DJ," like my favorite character from *Full House*. My first entry was simple, proclaiming:

> *Deer DJ,*
> *You will be my frend. I have a love for animils. I feel very sad for all the peepol who are poor.*
> *Love, Sarah*

Of course, as time went on, my entries became more advanced (and so did my spelling skills!). I started to write about my true desires, hopes, and fears. I turned to my journal when I needed to sort out problems and make sense of life. My journal became "the key to my soul," a utensil that opened up doors to reveal new aspects of my identity.

WHY SHOULD I KEEP A JOURNAL?

The benefits of journaling are boundless. Journals can be channels for creativity, especially if you like writing stories, poetry, or songs. For those of us who are easily worried and overwhelmed, getting our troubles down on paper makes them look infinitely smaller. Writing is great therapy. When you feel you have no one else to confide in, journals can be the perfect place to turn. As the young Anne Frank wrote in her famous diary, "I must tell someone and you are the best one to tell, as I know that, come what may, you always keep a secret."

Journals are also great documents of growth. Looking back on old journal entries is one of my favorite things to do; I can observe my development and learn from past experiences. Your journal will help you reflect on your soul searching growth and measure just how far you have come.

Most important, the exercises recommended in this chapter will help you articulate your emotions and get in the habit of self-expression. When we write, we are forced to find words to fit our souls, to verbalize our unique experiences. If we are truly honest with ourselves, journals will keep us in touch with our innermost fears and longings. This is the essence of soul searching!

Choosing a Journal

The great thing about keeping a journal is that there are so many ways to do it. Your journal can be a place to record your emotions, daily happenings, poetry, lists, quotes, artwork, and anything else you choose. Your journal can be a fancy leather diary, a binder filled with loose-leaf paper, or an inexpensive spiral notebook. You can write in your journal every day, on special occasions, or at random times in your life. You can choose to keep your work private, or you can share it with others.

Journals are like people; they come in many shapes, colors, and sizes, and every journal has a personality. When choosing one, make sure it is compatible with your individual style. For example, last year for Christmas I received a dazzling, exquisite journal that was painted with lilies and looked fit for a queen. However, when I tried to write in it, I discovered that I focused more on creating well-structured, neatly written entries than I did on expressing my real feelings. I bought a cheap, bright magenta journal, and I found myself free to write anything and everything that came to mind!

Three Important Tips

Although the first rule in journaling is that there are no rules, a few things have helped me in my journal journeys. Here are some suggestions to keep in mind:

1. Your journal is for you! You don't have to share it with anyone unless you choose to do so.

2. Don't censor yourself. Write what you feel, not what you think you should be feeling or wish you were feeling. There is no need to sound cool, sophisticated, or intelligent when you are writing in your private journal. When you write, make an effort to silence your inner critic and let your thoughts flow.

3. Don't worry about grammar, spelling, etc. It's fine to make these types of mistakes, since your English teacher isn't looking over your shoulder and shaking her head. Let this be a time to unwind and focus on self-expression, not grammar. At times you may not even want to write in complete sentences. Instead, just list phrases and ideas as they come to you.

Privacy

Feeling assured that your journal is private can make it easier to tell the truth. If you feel you are writing for an audience and not being completely honest, what's the point? Therefore, figuring out how to keep your journal safe is an important task. If you have a snoopy sibling or parent, it is smart to get a lock for your journal and find a secret storage place. Even if you trust your family, it is still a good idea to keep your journal out of sight. When you leave it in plain view, you tempt people who normally might never consider invading your privacy.

SPECIAL JOURNALS

Along with the look of your journal, you should decide what *kind* of journal you want to keep. Some people keep journals in which they record their daily activities. Others prefer to write sporadically. Personally, I keep several journals. Each one is different. For example, I have one for my everyday feelings in which I record what's going on in my life. I have another in which I practice my writing skills and keep short stories, poetry, and article ideas. Another journal records all of the *major* events in my life, from getting my period to starting high school.

I enjoy having different journals to match my different moods, but this technique won't work for everyone. If the idea appeals to your creative side, then give it a try. On the other hand, you might prefer having a close affinity with one journal at a time.

There are infinite types of journals you can keep, aside from the traditional "What I Thought About Today" type. The following are several ideas for unique journals:

The Visual Journal: This journal is perfect if you like the *idea* of keeping a journal, but you hate to write. In an artist's journal, you can use pictures, diagrams, collage, photos, stuff from your pockets, and whatever else you like to express what's on your mind.

The Gratitude Journal: Before you go to bed each night, write five things you were grateful for that day. The smell of your mom's perfume when you hugged her, or that delicate hummingbird you saw on your way to school are perfect examples. Your list needn't be spectacular. After all, simple pleasures are often the most meaningful.

The "Bits and Pieces" Journal: Once or twice a day, I see something that makes me laugh or sheds light on a problem I've been having. It may be a conversation at the lunch table, a picture in the newspaper, or the creative title of a book. A "Bits and Pieces" journal is a place to collect these little tid-bits of life. Write down that hilarious joke your best friend whispered to you during the school assembly. Photocopy that inspiring quote or poem in your English book. Cut out that picture in *National Geographic*. A "Bits and Pieces" journal is like an immense collage of experiences, memories, and thoughts.

The Question Journal: If you enjoy philosophical thinking and like to put your thoughts down on paper, the "Question Journal" is a perfect way to do this. Each time you want to make an entry, write a question at the top of the page. You might ask yourself, for example, "Is there a God?" or "How can I improve my relationship with my parents?" Then, try to answer the question. It may help to approach the problem with several different answers. You don't have to decide on a definite answer, just consider the possibilities.

The Travel Journal: If you love to take trips, you may want to start a special journal just for your travels and vacations. Write about the places you see, the people you meet, and what you learn from the trips. Include memorabilia like airplane tickets if you want to.

The Creativity Journal: This is a place to collect anything that fires your creativity—poems, story ideas, quotes, etc. This will become a record of the artist within you.

The People Journal: Relationships with family and friends are often on a teenager's mind. This journal is a place to record the progress of all the relationships in your life. Write about the great conversation you had with your dad, the fight with your best friend, and your struggles with the boy you like. Get all your emotions out, but this is one journal to keep under lock and key!

The Everything Journal: The various types of journals above are just springboards for your own ideas. You don't have to limit your journal to only one type. You can keep a journal filled with art, quotes, questions, gratitude, and ANYTHING YOU WANT!

Okay, now let's get to work. . .

JOURNALING ACTIVITIES

When I want to write in my journal but can't think of anything to write about, I use journaling activities. The following is a list of eight journaling activities that will get your creative juices flowing.

1. Write a "Me List." This is a list of 100 adjectives that describe you. Yes, I said 100! Why so many? Well, the first few you write will probably be the generic things you've always considered yourself to be: talkative or shy, athletic or klutzy. But I want you to get past these words that have always labeled you. Once you get past number 50 or so, your mind will be challenged to divulge less prominent, but equally important, aspects of your personality. Get to know yourself.

2. *Write a Letter to Yourself.* Sometimes I wonder if I'll be able to recall certain experiences from my adolescence. Will I remember the jittery first day of my freshman year in enough detail to tell my children? Will I be able to lie in bed when I'm 90 years old and chuckle at the time I was Pipi Longstocking for Halloween? These are moments that I never want to forget, but how can I reassure myself that I won't? I decided that writing a letter to myself was the solution.

Once a year, on a special occasion such as your birthday, write a letter to yourself. In this letter, you can reflect on the past year, state your goals for the coming year, and simply remind yourself of who you really are and want to be. One year later, read your letter and write a new one. Writing letters to yourself is the perfect way to keep track of how you and your goals change over the years.

You don't have to wait for your birthday to write a letter to yourself. You can write a letter to be opened when you:

- ◎ graduate from high school
- ◎ get your first job
- ◎ meet your first boyfriend

The next time you are mad at your parents, write a letter to yourself that can be opened when *you* become a parent. Make a list of the things you like about the way you were raised, and the things you absolutely hate. If you ever have a child of your own, you can open this letter to remember which parenting techniques are actually helpful and which are just plain annoying!

3. *Switch It Up.* Despite the mystery and complexity that surround the human brain, the basics of Brain 101 aren't so tough to understand. Our brains operate in two hemispheres: the left and the right. Both sides have different functions. In most cases, the left hemisphere of the brain controls the right side of the body, and is also in charge of language skills, mathematical thinking, reasoning, and analysis. The right side of the brain controls the left side of the body, and directs your imagination, artistic skills, and intuition, among other things.

Although the right side of your brain is responsible for lots of cool and creative stuff, most people don't exercise it as much as they should. To get your right hemisphere working, write a journal entry with your non-dominant hand. You may be surprised at what the other side of your brain has to say. (Hint: it's often more negative at first, but also more revealing once you give it a chance.)

4. Deconstruct Your Myths. Everyone has myths about themselves. You may think you aren't a good public speaker, even though you nailed your oral report in history class. You may be under the impression that you could never be in the school chorus, despite the fact that you wail in awesome harmony with the radio (only when you're home alone, of course). Sometimes we create these myths for ourselves; other times we let the people around us dictate who we are and where our talents lie.

In first grade, I was one of the worst spellers in the class. Now that I am in high school, I still consider myself an awful speller, even though my spelling is better than the majority of my classmates. This is one of my personal myths. What are the myths that surround your identity? Label them, and give reasons why they aren't true. Figuring out our myths is the first step to dispelling them.

5. Emotion Commotion. In a moment of intense emotion, allow the feelings

What do YOU think?

One reason I keep a journal is so that when I'm all grown up, I can reread it and remember in greater detail all the things that happened to me at this age.
—EMMARIE HUETTEMAN, AGE 13

Journaling has allowed me to grow and define myself as a person, just like what doing arm curls would do for my biceps. There may be brief periods of realizing pain or soreness, but like the little muscle tears one gets from exercising, they only add to my strength.
—MOLLY BRANNAN, AGE 16

Journal writing started out as a hobby, but later developed into a therapeutic way for me to vent my feelings and explore who I am. Journaling helps me because it makes my emotions clearer—worries, thoughts, or memories always make more sense to me when I write them down. It is also helpful when I want to eternalize a special moment or event.
—JULIA HALPRIN JACKSON, AGE 16

I tend to keep a "traditional" diary. I keep it up because it lets me express myself, the way I feel, right at that moment, without facing consequences like hurting someone's feelings. I also keep a journal of possible storylines like Nathaniel Hawthorne used to do. If I hear an interesting conversation, I'll jot down some of it for my writing.
—GILLIAN McHALE, AGE 15

to wash over you. Savor them, taste them, then try to express them to your journal. Don't worry about complete sentences or things that make sense. Write down colors, visual images, and just showers of emotion as they come to you.

6. Simple Solutions. Think of a problem, situation, or event that frustrates or confuses you. Then start writing your emotions, feelings, and fears about it. Be very honest, even painfully so. Really analyze how you are feeling and why you feel that way. If you could do anything, how would things be different?

7. Rocky Relationships. Think about a relationship you want to understand better. Write about a key incident in that relationship. How does that person make you feel when you are around him/her? Why? In a perfect world, how would your relationship be different?

8. Get Inspiration From the Best. When you don't know what to write in your own journal, why not get inspiration from the best—teenage journal-keepers just like you? Several diaries by courageous teens have been published so that they are accessible to girls around the world. Among my favorites: *Anne Frank: Diary of a Young Girl* (a must-read!), *Go Ask Alice, Zlata's Diary,* and *It Happened to Nancy.* Although all of these diaries deal with serious issues in a painfully honest and often sad way, they can help us better understand ourselves and the power of journal keeping.

FINAL THOUGHTS

This has been a chapter full of ideas and suggestions, but nothing about journaling is set in stone. Your ideas are just as valid as mine, since anything goes in the land of journal keeping. Don't give up if you miss a few days, weeks, or even months in your journal. Consistent journaling will bring you in close touch with your emotions and experiences. The more you write, the more you'll love it! As Henry David Thoreau once said, "Direct your eye right inward, and you'll find a thousand regions in your mind yet undiscovered. Travel them, and be expert in home-cosmography." What an incredible journey!

RESOURCES

The Creative Journal for Teens: Making Friends With Yourself, by Lucia
    Capacchione

Through My Eyes: A Journal for Teens, by Linda Kranz

*Write Where You Are: How to Use Writing to Make Sense of Your
    Life: A Guide for Teens,* by Caryn Mirriam-Goldberg, Ph.D.

For more journaling ideas visit: www.writingthejourney.com

CHAPTER 6

Sleep On It

DREAM INTERPRETATION

One day at school, I revealed my secret desire to be a chart-topping singer. My friend laughed and replied, "In your dreams!" I thought about it for a moment, realizing the accuracy of his advice. Becoming a Mariah Carey of sorts may have been an unrealistic goal for me, but when it comes to my dreams, I can go anywhere, do anything, and be anyone I desire. Dreams are awesome playgrounds for the inner genius, and they deserve our respect and attention.

Scientists are still not 100 percent sure why we dream, but they think it helps the brain sort out problems and tensions from our waking lives. Through an intricate coding method, our subconscious creates a script for our dreams that can help us release pent up feelings, brainstorm solutions to daily dilemmas, and bring previously unrecognized skills to our attention. Some of the greatest insights into our identities are revealed in the language of dreams. Dreams are windows into our souls, and they have important messages for us. When we listen to our dreams, we get a glimpse into the mysterious terrain of the subconscious. When you pay attention, you will be amazed at what this complex part of you has to say! Our dreams arrive each night like letters from a dear friend offering advice and counsel. Why would you leave a letter like that unopened?

A HISTORY OF DREAMS

People have been interested in dreams since the beginning of time. The first dream interpretation book was created by the Egyptians in 1300 B.C. Many famous inventions, works of literature, and scientific theories were inspired by dreams. For example, the idea for Mary Shelley's famous book, *Frankenstein*, came from a dream she had when she was nineteen. Albert Einstein developed his theory of relativity through a dream he had as a teenager. Many famous authors and artists, from Anne Rice to Stephen King to Salvador Dali, attribute some of their greatest works to their dreams. If these people learned to harness the power and creativity of their dreams, maybe you can do the same!

Most people have between three and six dreams each night, each one lasting between 10 and 45 minutes. Most dreams take place during a certain stage of sleep called Rapid Eye Movement (REM) sleep. This phase starts about 90 minutes after you first fall asleep, and continues in more frequent cycles as the night progresses. This is when your magnificent brain is converted into a movie theater, showing spectacular shows written, produced, edited, and acted out by YOU!

REMEMBERING YOUR DREAMS

Despite the fact that we have about 500,000 dreams in our lifetimes, it is estimated that we remember only five percent of them. So if we compare our brains to movie theaters, how can we get "front row seats" to view our dreams more clearly? Remembering our dreams is easier than we might expect, once the habit is formed. Years ago, I had a hard time remembering my dreams, but now it's almost impossible for me to *forget* them! How did I acquire this skill? By writing down my dreams every morning in a dream journal.

Dream Journals

The vital, all-important secret to becoming a dream expert lies in **keeping a dream journal!** Dream journals convert the abstract, mystical world inside your head into tangible, organized ideas on paper, which are much easier to understand. Here's how to get started:

1. First, pick out a dream journal. It can be whatever you choose: a plain pad of paper, a fancy diary, or anything else you want. Place your journal, along with a pen or pencil, beside your bed.

2. Before going to sleep, open your journal to a fresh page and jot down some notes about your day (big events, problems, fights, gossip). Repeat the following sentence out loud: "I will remember my dreams." Though you might feel a bit kooky saying it, this sentence signals your brain that you care about your dreams and want to understand them. This will make your subconscious more likely to cooperate.

3. As soon as you wake up in the morning, try to remember your dreams. Stay in your bed with your journal and write down anything and everything you can remember. Don't worry if you can't recall the entire dream. Often, just writing down the parts you can remember causes more of the dream to come back to you. Writing in the present tense (I am climbing the beanstalk) instead of the past tense (I climbed the beanstalk) can help you feel more involved in the action of the dream, which might jolt your memory.

4. When you write about your dream, try to include detailed descriptions of where you were, what you felt, and what you saw/smelled/heard. Don't worry about spelling or grammar when you write.

5. If you don't have time to record your dream in the morning, at least try to jot down a few key words or phrases to help you remember the dream later on. You can do this in less than a minute.

6. After writing the narrative of the dream, use the opposite page of your journal to record how you felt about the dream. This part is incredibly important. Think about the emotions you experienced during and after the dream, and write down anything in real life that the dream might relate to.

7. If you would like, give your dream a title. Try to summarize the dream in a few sentences below the title. Date each dream, so that you can look back on it and remember when it occurred.

SOLVING THE MYSTERY

Okay, so now you know how to remember your dreams and record them. But what use is that if you don't know what they're trying to tell you? To unlock the meaning, remember that each person, place, or object in your dreams is representative of something. Understanding the messages enshrined in these objects is a bit like playing detective. You must hunt down the answers to what journalists call "the Five W's": who, what, when, where, and why.

Who? Who are the characters in your dream? What do these people mean to you in real life? What do they symbolize? Let's say that, for example, your grandmother appeared in a dream. What does she represent? If she is sick or weak in real life, she could be a symbol of fragility. If she is a very warm and loving person, she could symbolize compassion or wisdom.

What? Make a list of all the objects in your dream. What do these things represent? You can get a dream dictionary from the library to help, but you must also use your own wisdom. No one else can interpret a dream for you, since *each of us has our own unique experiences.* For example, you may consider dogs to be very friendly, comforting symbols, while your best friend may associate them with danger and fear. To get started, refer to the list of common dream symbols at the end of this chapter.

When? When did this dream take place in the context of your life? Are you going through any special changes right now? Dreams usually correspond to the events taking place in your waking life. If you are moving to a new house, starting a new school, or breaking up with a boyfriend, this is likely to be reflected in your dream.

Where? Where a dream takes place is a crucial part of its meaning. For example, a dream that takes place in an airplane could be a hint that you're feeling "on top of the world." Of course, if the plane is about to crash, it could mean that your hopes about something recently took a nose dive. A house often represents your self, with each room being a different aspect of your personality.

Why? This is the most important of the "Five W's." Considering the answers to the four main questions above, why do you think your subconscious sent you this dream? What is the meaning of it?

Sample Dream Interpretation

Let me show you an example of how I interpreted one of my own dreams. In the dream, I was baby-sitting a young, adorable toddler. When I turned my back on her for a split second, she climbed a ladder to the attic and sneaked into a small hole. I saw her and tried to follow, but I couldn't fit in the hole. She sat inside it, having a wonderful time, reading her books and laughing. I was frightened, because I knew I was responsible for her. She peaked down at me, and said, "It's a great dilemma: you want to protect me, but you want to set me free. You want to see me fly, but you don't want me to be hurt." (Yes, I know toddlers don't talk like this, but it's a dream!) In the end, I knew it was best to let her stay in the hole, but to keep watching her from the ladder.

The first thing I did was list all of the important symbols in the dream, and what they could represent:

Symbols

Me (baby-sitter): responsible, concerned, parent-like

Toddler: young, creative, inner child

Hole: height, freedom, fun, independence

Ladder: gateway between responsibility and freedom

Dream Meaning: Using this list of symbols, I put my feelings about the dream together to figure out its meaning. I decided that the dream deals with the issue of my own "coming of age." As a fifteen-year-old, I was struggling with the paradox of adolescence: wanting the sheltered innocence of childhood, but also desiring the freedom of adulthood. I think the dream was telling me that I should let my creative side (the little girl) be free and unleashed, but I should also protect my innocence. I can do this by staying in the middle ground, on the "ladder" between dependency and freedom.

Common Teen Dreams

Although we all have our own unique set of dreams each night, some symbolic dreams are shared by many people, probably because they deal with universal issues like insecurity and joy. The following are some common teen dreams:

Being Chased: This probably signifies the existence of something you don't want to face up to. What, in real life, are you trying to escape from? A fight with your parents? A bad grade? This dream is warning you to turn around and face your problems, or else they will catch up to you in an unpleasant manner. When you run from your worries, they grow in strength and power. If you confront your fears, they usually shrink down much smaller than you imagined them to be.

Drowning: Help! You may be feeling that you're in over your head. This dream often results from sensations of emotional overload and helplessness. Try to pinpoint the reason you feel overwhelmed. Is it your inability to say "no" when someone asks a favor of you? Is it too many activities and responsibilities in your hands? Are you too stressed? The purpose of dreams is to bring problems like this to your attention, so you can fix whatever is off balance in your life.

Flying: My favorite dream! Flying symbolizes joy, optimism, freedom, and confidence. Have you achieved something great lately? This dream is usually a pleasant signal that you're headed in the right direction.

Maze: This usually represents a descent into the unconscious. In other words, a trip in a maze may mean you are searching the interiors of your soul for something that your conscious ego is attempting to hide. On the other hand, it may represent feelings of confusion and a lack of direction.

Masks: These can be a symbol for the various ways in which we are forced to obscure our true identities. If you find yourself unable to remove a mask in your dream, this may reflect an inability to express yourself in your waking life. If someone else is forcing you to wear a mask, you may feel as though the outside world is causing you to "mask" your real feelings.

Nudity: One of the most classic dreams involves finding yourself in a public place . . . unclothed or otherwise physically revealed! This may reflect feelings of vulnerability under the close scrutiny of others. However, if you are enjoying your nudity, it may indicate a desire to shed defenses or free your authentic self.

Violence: If you are a victim of violence in your dream, particularly self-inflicted violence, it may indicate a sense of guilt or desire to be held accountable for a wrongdoing. Violence towards others in dreams often represents a battle between the dreamer's conscious and subconscious mind. It might also reflect a desire to be more assertive.

Common Dream Symbols

If you're at a loss for understanding your dreams, dream symbols can also help you decode uncharted territory. Common objects, colors, and numbers all have symbolic meanings in a dream. Though dream symbols can be helpful, ultimately only you can decide what these symbols mean in your dreams. Here are just a few common dream symbols:

Moon: This common dream symbol often represents femininity and serenity. It can also emphasize cycles.

Death: Dreaming about death can mean that something is coming to an end or that there will be a new beginning. Death in a dream can also symbolize future change.

Keys: Keys, as long as they're not lost or broken, can symbolize financial, personal, and social success.

Houses: Houses often reflect the self. The rooms in the house represent different parts of your self. A dream that takes place in the attic might symbolize the dreamer's spiritual development, while a dream that takes place in the basement might represent your subconscious.

Storms: Storms in dreams can symbolize sudden changes, emotional turmoil, and a feeling of being out of control.

Teeth: Many people dream about their teeth falling out. This can often symbolize that the dreamer is experiencing difficulty having her voice heard, that she is shy, or is feeling unacknowledged.

Telephones: A telephone can symbolize a message from the subconscious, and should be closely examined.

Dream Colors

Pink: love

Red: passion, anger, or danger

Black: the unconscious mind, death

Gray: fear, confusion

White: peace, truth, purity, can also symbolize death

Green: positive change, healing, growth, newness, jealousy

Blue: openness, spirituality, sadness

Yellow: peacefulness, hope, intellect, cowardice

Brown: earthiness, depression

Dream Numbers

One: individuality, unity, completeness

Two: partners, twins

Three: trinity, the body-mind-spirit, trilogy, self-exploration

Four: limitations, earthly things

Five: changes, harmony

Recurring Dreams . . . and Nightmares!

Every once in a while, a certain image or theme might appear repeatedly in your dreams. This is called a recurring dream, and it is usually a very significant window into your self. Recurring dreams happen for a reason: the brain is trying to send us a very important message. It will send that message, over and over, until we listen.

Recurring dreams often come in the form of nightmares. Although they are no fun, it is important to write these dreams down in as much detail as possible. Then, you must study the dream and try to decode its message. Once the meaning of a nightmare becomes clear, try to deal with the problem in real life. If we confront our bad dreams by acknowledging their importance and attempting to understand them, they are more likely to disappear. After having a nightmare, I often like to recreate the dream in my imagination while I'm awake, creating a more favorable outcome.

To discourage nightmares, you might consider starting a soothing bedtime routine. Avoid caffeinated sodas and chocolate; drink warm chamomile tea instead. Try to eat dinner as early as possible, and avoid snacks after 9 p.m. Some girls have special rituals they complete before bed, from reading a book to taking a warm bath. Having a regular schedule and going to sleep around the same time every night can also help.

DREAM ON

What do YOU think?

I have a very interesting book about dream symbols and I have found it useful in deciphering my dreams. For example, I dreamed of mice and when I looked in the book it explained that mice mean disappointment. The strange thing is, that is what I had been feeling lately.

—TANYA COLLINGS, AGE 14

My recurring dream is of me walking through the snow. My parents keep pushing me down so I'm covered in snow. I think my dream probably signifies the high-pressure I feel from the expectations my parents have for me, and sometimes it is a bit overwhelming.

—CAROLINE GIBSON, AGE 16

I think recurring dreams and nightmares are ways for the mind to vent emotions freely that might be kept inside while the person is awake. The way you analyze a dream depends on if you are looking at the bigger picture or not.

—EMMARIE HUETTEMAN, AGE 13

I hope that this chapter has helped you to see just how much our dreams have to offer us as soul searchers. As you continue to seek to understand your dreams, you will find an incredible power to help you in your everyday life. Trust what your subconscious has to teach you, and you will be amazed at what you will find!

RESOURCES

Cloud Nine: A Dreamer's Dictionary, by Sandra A. Thomson

Dreams: Unlock the Secrets of Your Subconscious, by Frank Garfield and Rhonda Stewart-Garfield

Dreams Can Help: A Journal Guide to Understanding Your Dreams and Making Them Work for You, by Jonni Kincher

The Dream Sourcebook: A Guide to the Theory and Interpretation of Dreams, by Phyllis Koch-Sheras, Ph.d. and Amy Lemley

The Hidden Power of Dreams: How to Use Dreams on Your Spiritual Journey, by Denise Linn

The Secret Language of Dreams: A Visual Key to Their Meanings, by David Fontana

For a complete dream dictionary on-line, visit: www.swoon.com/dream/index.html

CHAPTER 7

Cultivate Your Passions

WHAT DO YOU LOVE?

Imagine you are walking down the cereal aisle of the supermarket when you over-hear a conversation between two friendly-looking people. They seem to feel strong-ly about what they are discussing; they also seem very knowledgeable. The topic of their conversation excites you so much that you can't resist introducing yourself and joining in.

In this short exercise, what is it the two strangers were talking about that thrilled you? Is it an activity you've loved since you were young? Is it a topic you learned about or researched in school? Or maybe something you always pledged you would do if you had more time? Whatever you envisioned the conversation to be about is probably a clue to **your own personal passion**.

Most of us have great ideas about what we would do, if only we had the time, the money, or the willpower. Soul searching is all about finding those great ideas, shedding our inhibitions, and going after what we truly desire. When we're doing what we really love and feel passionate about, we are truly in touch with our souls. Think about how you feel when you're doing something you really love. This is an important key to who you are. Sometimes it can be easy to let fear, indecisiveness, or reticence stand in our way, but life is most rewarding when we learn to follow our dreams. As Thoreau said, "If one advances confidently in the direction of his dreams, and endeavors to live the life which he has imagined, he will meet with a success unexpected in common hours."

One person who inspires me is a substitute science teacher I had once named Melissa. As a teenager, Melissa became completely absorbed by her interest in biology. She was especially fascinated by primates. Instead of sitting in her room thinking about how cool monkeys were, she called the zoo and made arrangements to volunteer. After a year of working there, she met an expert researcher who became her mentor. Eventually, her lifelong dream came true, and she went to the rainforest to research monkeys. She is now a professional scientist who loves her job. What would her life be like now if she hadn't taken that first step and acted on her passion?

POSSIBLE PASSIONS

Each and every passion is unique, like Melissa's love for monkeys or my brother's enjoyment of collecting PEZ dispensers. Your passions may be strange and quirky, or they may be quite ordinary. It really doesn't matter, as long as a certain topic captivates you, inspires you, or gives you joy. It was always easy for me to tell that I was passionate about writing; my bookshelf is filled with technique books, I go to poetry readings and book signings whenever I can, and I escape daily into the pages of my journal. But for many people, finding their passion isn't so crystal clear. Others struggle with having passion for many topics! And unfortunately, a few people *never* figure it out. Don't let that be you!

Just as there are many different passions to choose from, there are many ways to *fulfill* a passion, as well. Some of your loves may take you to a job or even a lifelong career. You may choose to develop others into rewarding hobbies or pastimes. Even if your passion doesn't dominate your future, you can still derive enjoyment and pleasure from honoring what you love. For example, I know a woman whose girlhood fantasy was to be a singer. But as she grew up, her main goals changed and she found a career she liked even more than music. However, she never forgot her dream and still practiced singing every chance she got. Then, at her wedding, she planned a big surprise and serenaded her new husband along with the band and her best friends as backup. It was her moment to be the rock star she always dreamed of! You just never know how your dreams may express themselves.

So, what do you feel passionate about? What do you love doing? What adult jobs intrigue you? What problems in the world bother you? Take a moment to brainstorm and write down your passions. Don't worry if this doesn't come easily to you. Some people immediately know their passion, but with others it takes lots of time, patience, and thought. On the other hand, you may have lots of things you're passionate about. This list is certainty not limited to one topic!

What do YOU think?

I really want to be a published author, and maybe write screenplays and breed dogs, too. I've kept a journal, been published in a national kid's magazine, kept on writing, and started a writing workshop for elementary school kids.

—LIZA BIRNBAUM, AGE 12

Being a political science buff, I think I'd have a lot of fun as a political journalist, much like one of my female idols, Molly Ivins. For my political ambitions, I followed the 2000 presidential campaign extensively and enjoyed doing it. I read articles and watch TV with people, mostly women, with similar jobs as my dream.

—GILLIAN McHALE, AGE 15

I would like to write screenplays because good movies can move like poetry, flowing and beautiful, with meaning and thought behind them.

—CAITLIN DWYER, AGE 16

My dream for the future is to either become a cardiovascular surgeon or WNBA player. I play basketball on two teams during the summer and I love practicing outside. Also for my other dream, I study hard at life science.

—NICOLE NORTON, AGE 13

What is Smart?

While you are considering your passions, keep your own unique talents in mind. While talent and passion may not *always* overlap, we usually enjoy doing things we are good at. Unfortunately, school can sometimes send us negative messages about our intelligence and abilities. But did you know there are many different types of intelligence? Scientists have identified seven intelligence types so far, yet school usually only tests us on two or three of these! The human brain has a vast capacity for knowledge. Our brilliance can manifest itself in our artistic intellect, our ability to communicate, our reasoning skills, and our physical coordination. And *all* of these intelligence types are valued and rewarded in different areas of the working world. Howard Gardner, author of *Frames of Mind: The Theory of Multiple Intelligences*, identifies the following seven main types of intelligence:

Linguistic Intelligence is the skill for writing, speaking, and listening. Authors, public speakers, and politicians use linguistic intelligence in their work.

Musical Intelligence is the ability to make sense of musical concepts like rhythm, pitch, and composition. Singers, instrumentalists, composers, and dancers must have strong musical intelligence.

Logical-Mathematical Intelligence indicates an ease with numbers and quantity comprehension. Reasoning skills are very important for this type of intelligence, which is often found in scientists and mathematicians.

Spatial Intelligence means that a person has strong visual perception skills. For example, she can easily imagine a complex object, rotate it mentally, and see it from various angles. Artists, engineers, and chess players have very keen spatial abilities.

Bodily-Kinesthetic Intelligence makes a person skilled at controlling physical movements. This can include speed, hand-eye coordination, flexibility, etc. Athletes, dancers, and mime artists specialize in this type of intelligence.

Interpersonal Intelligence is the talent of good communication with others. In their social interactions, people with interpersonal intelligence have an easy time anticipating others' wants and needs. Psychologists and teachers are especially skilled in this area.

Intrapersonal Intelligence pertains to a thorough understanding of oneself. If you are skilled in this respect, you probably take strong notice of your own feelings and the emotions of those around you. Religious leaders and politicians have high intrapersonal intelligence.

According to Gardner, each of us has varying levels of ability in each of these categories. By evaluating our talents in these areas, we can assess the skills we want to develop, as well as those which we want to celebrate. Why not give each of your intelligences a chance to shine every once in a while? And once you figure out your unique areas of expertise, pursue them with intensity and let them guide you toward success.

FEEDING YOUR PASSION

Passions are a bit like plants: we need to feed them and provide them with the right environment if we want them to grow. How can you feed your passion?

⊚ Surround yourself with friends and family who are supportive of your pursuits.

- Join a group or club that is organized around your passion.
- Find a role model who shares your passion.
- Read books and watch movies about it.
- Practice!

Here are some ideas for developing several common passions:

Art: If you are an art lover, visit as many museums and art exhibits as possible. Take classes at school or from a community college in your area. Explore the different mediums of art: drawing, painting, sculpture, photography, etc. Pay special attention to unusual and interesting art forms (which may not be as highly publicized or easily accessible), like printmaking or trash sculpting. If you happen to know an artist personally, ask if you could visit his or her studio and quietly observe him or her at work for a day.

Nature: Do you love animals? The great outdoors? Get involved with an environmental group like the Audubon Society, the Sierra Club or Greenpeace. If animals are your cup of tea, try volunteering at your local zoo or animal shelter. These groups really need your help and you can learn a lot about animals, environmental issues, and even future careers for yourself.

Music: There are millions of ways to enjoy music. You can listen to it, play it, sing it, attend concerts, etc. Try experiencing music in every way you can think of. Dig through your dad's old records or buy a CD from the "International" section of the music store. Listen for the music of everyday life: the sound of rain on your ceiling, the chatter of birds in the morning, the "goo-goo, gaa-gaa" of your baby sister. If you enjoy performing, get a gig at a local coffee shop or do a number at the school talent show. It might be fun to start a band with some friends or record tapes of your music to give as gifts.

Science: Join the science club at school. Hundreds of organizations hold science-related contests for teens each year, ranging from general knowledge competitions like the National Science Bowl to more specific awards like the National Young Astronomer Award. Ask your favorite science teacher to sponsor you in entering one of these science fairs or contests. Over the summer, look for volunteering opportunities at science labs, hospitals, etc.

Sports: Whatever sport you enjoy, set goals for yourself. Working toward simple, realistic goals will help you push harder and reach new athletic heights. Learn more about a particular athlete you admire, and follow his or her career. A great way to spend time with friends and family while feeding your passion is to attend sporting events together or even organizing family games. Technique books and videos from the library can also inspire you. However, none of these tips will do more for you than lots of good old-fashioned *practice!*

Writing: No matter what type of writing you like best, all authors benefit from being exposed to different genres. Read as much as you can, and as many different types of books as you can. Keep a journal in which you jot down interesting phrases and story ideas. Most important, sit down and write *at least once a week.* When you complete a poem, story, or whatever, find a trusted adult or a friend who is willing to read and critique it. Don't be insulted by this type of advice; every writer has room to improve. If you do get published someday, you'll have to work with an editor, so you might as well learn how now. After you've polished your piece, you may want to send your work to a newspaper, magazine, literary journal, or book publisher in hopes of being published.

Unusual Interests

If you have an interest that isn't shared by many other kids, following your passion can sometimes feel lonely. I know a boy who tap-dances professionally. He is very successful, but sometimes jealous kids crack jokes and tease him about it. He doesn't let it bother him much because he knows he's following his heart. If you have an interest that makes you feel isolated, chances are there is someone out there feeling the same way. Search the Internet for chat rooms or look for newsletters about your passion. If you feel inspired to teach other people about your interest, hold an information seminar at school, or start a club to teach others.

SUPPORTING YOUR PASSION

Clubs or interest groups are a great way to feed your passion. At these groups you can meet people with similar interests. Joining a club organized around your love is especially important if your friends and family don't share your passion. It can be very motivating to realize that other people find bird watching as fascinating as you do! Also, you will benefit from other's advice and experience. Groups renew our energy and inspire us. They give us a place to exchange ideas and brainstorm.

So where do you find the right club for you? Start at your school. Does it have an art club you can join? If not, try contacting stores that specialize in your passion. For instance, a music store may be able to tell you about guitar clubs in the area. Also try searching on the Internet for virtual support groups. (Did you know there is a website for people who love to collect sand?) Finally, consider taking classes at community colleges in your area. This can be a great place to meet others who can tell you about support groups you may not know about. If all else fails, you can always start your own club—it isn't as hard as it sounds!

Start Your Own Club

The first step to launching a new club is getting the word out. You may want to include only three or four close friends in your club, or you may decide to look for members throughout your school, city, or state. Make some flyers to hand out among prospective members, and ask your friends to spread the word. Post a sign-up sheet where interested people can write their names, phone numbers, and e-mail addresses.

Once you've gathered a list of kids, pick a convenient place and time for your first meeting. At this meeting, plan to discuss your goals for the club. It is helpful to have a mission statement by which the club will operate; this gives members a sense of purpose vital to the club's success. If you think the group is large enough, consider appointing club officers, such as president, vice president, secretary, etc. Establish whether or not your club will need money to handle expenses such as crafts or field trips. If so, you may wish to designate a treasurer who will handle the club's money and think of fundraising ideas. At the end of the meeting, make sure you have an agenda for the future that suits everyone's needs. If your club members are enthusiastic and dedicated, you will be able to support each other's dreams while having lots of fun.

Clubs Can Change the World

Don't believe that your passion club can change the world? Large, prestigious groups like the National Organization for Women and Amnesty International may have lots of members and political clout, but they aren't the only ones making a difference. Clubs can turn into powerful organizations. Many kids clubs, even small ones, have done big things.

In Somerville, Massachusetts, eight kids joined up with television director Roberto Arevalo to do something they called the Mirror Project. The kids explored their inner-city neighborhood with video cameras, making movies that painted a fascinating picture of their lives. The movie won several awards. Thanks to their work, the U.S. Department of Housing and Urban Development has chosen to continue their program at community centers around town.

Using the Internet and a monthly newsletter, a group called "The Clean and Green Club" has been helping kids learn about the environment and fight against pollution. Started by a ten-year-old girl named Marielle, the club gives members tons of ideas on how to care for Mother Earth. Thanks to Marielle's website, over 15,000 kids have been able to unite in an effort to help the Earth!

START PLANNING

Whatever your passion is, start thinking of how to nurture it. Think of three ways you plan to feed your passion in the next month:

1._____

_____

2._____

_____

3._____

_____

THINK OUTSIDE THE BOX

One thing to remember about passions: don't get boxed in. Remember that just because you love collecting dolls or shooting hoops *now* doesn't mean you have to devote the rest of your life to it. People's interests change over time; you don't have to love the same thing forever. Every once in a while, take time to reassess your passions and set new goals for yourself. Explore what you love in your journal, and record new interests as they enter your life. This world is full of endless passion opportunities!

RESOURCES

Better Than a Lemonade Stand! Small Business Ideas for Kids by Daryl Bernstein (age 15)

Career Ideas for Nature Lovers and Other Outdoor Types, by Theresa Foy DiGeronimo

Career Ideas for Kids Who Like Art, by Diane Lindsey Reeves

Career Ideas for Kids Who Like Science, by Diane Lindsey Reeves

Careers for Women Who Love Sports, by Robin Roberts

Cool Careers for Girls series, by Ceel Pasternak

Create A Life that Tickles Your Soul: Finding Peace, Passion, & Purpose, by Suzanne Willis Zoglio, Ph.D.

Frames of Mind: The Theory of Multiple Intelligences, by Howard Gardner

Name Your Passion: A User's Guide to Finding Your Personal Purpose, by Paul Kordis and Susan Kordis

So You Wanna Be a Rock Star? by Stephen Anderson

So You Wanna Be a Writer? by Vicky Hamilton & Cathleen Greenwood

CHAPTER 8

Create Good Karma

HELPING OTHERS, HELPING YOURSELF

From 1953 until her death in 1981, a woman known as "Peace Pilgrim" spread love across America. Despite her graying hair and wrinkling skin, she spent the last years of her life walking thousands of miles across the country, trying to deliver a message of compassion and perseverance. Peace Pilgrim has a lot to teach our generation of girls. "We are all cells in the body of humanity," she once wrote. "Each one has a contribution to make, and we'll know from within what this contribution is. . ."

Have you made your contribution yet? Are you ready? Service to others is a vital part of the soul searching process. As we work to serve others, we simultaneously work to discover ourselves. With each kind word and generous action, we nourish our own hearts as much as the receiver's. Through service, we start to observe our inner strength. We see how much impact a single girl can have on the world, which builds our sense of purpose, confidence, and faith. As Peace Pilgrim advised, "No one can find inner peace except by working, not in a self-centered way, but for the whole human family."

THE LAW OF KARMA

To understand the importance of volunteering, it can help to explore an Eastern principle known as "karma." The word itself translates to mean "work" or "action," but it has much broader implications. The law of karma is similar to the principle of cause and effect: we get back whatever we put in.

Good deeds and thoughtful actions bring positive benefits to all areas of our lives, while harmful actions have a detrimental effect on our souls.

The law of karma encourages us to devote our time and energy unselfishly to people, places, and things in need. We're forced to forget our egos for a moment and humble ourselves before issues of greater importance. After spending the day working in a homeless shelter, it probably won't seem like such a horrifying trauma if your crush catches you picking your nose! The law of karma helps us put things into perspective.

Yet in a funny way, it also gives us permission to be a tiny bit selfish in our motivations for volunteering. After all, the law of karma promises that we'll feel better about ourselves and improve our own lives with each good deed we do. Even Mahatma Gandhi admitted that his main objective in helping the poor was "to serve no one but myself, to find my own self-realization through . . . service."

Of course, it is important to keep our intentions as pure as possible whenever we're volunteering. It's easy to do kind things with the anticipation of rewards, recognition, or compliments in the forefront of our minds. A number of kids these days do community service merely to impress college admission officers or fulfill school requirements. Sure, this type of service is better than nothing, but it's not as rewarding as it could be. In order to make volunteering an integral part of our soul searching quest, we must let go of our egos and give from our hearts.

KARMA IN NATURE

Some of the best examples of karma in action are found in nature. The two seas of Israel are a perfect case in point. The Sea of Galilee is a sparkling body of water filled with splashing fish and surrounded by lush vegetation. On the other hand, no life can survive in or around the Dead Sea because it is so salty. Although these neighboring seas receive healthy water from the same source, the difference between the two is amazing!

What could possibly be the reason for this vast difference between the Sea of Galilee and the Dead Sea? The secret, as author Bruce Barton points out, is that the Sea of Galilee takes in the waters of the Jordan River, but allows water to flow out as well. It gives and receives equally. The Dead Sea, however, only takes in the Jordan's water, never letting any flow out. By holding in all it is given, the Dead Sea poisons itself.

Haven't you noticed that karma works the same way in our own lives? Often, the more self-absorbed and egocentric we become, the less we gain. We think we're helping ourselves by acting selfishly, but on the contrary, we've forgotten that the more we give, the more we receive. Since soul searching is a deeply internal process, we must struggle to remind ourselves that reaching out to others is an integral part of our inner journey.

WHERE TO BEGIN

You don't need to devote your whole life to charity in order to make a difference. You don't need to be the next Mother Teresa or Gandhi. If you feel ready to begin volunteering, it's probably best to start small. Begin by paying attention to the little opportunities for giving throughout the day. On your way home from school tomorrow, bring a big plastic bag to collect litter in, or make a pledge to smile at everyone you pass. These tiny deeds will make you feel better about yourself while getting your volunteer muscles revved up.

When you're ready to get more involved, the real challenge begins. You've got to find a cause that suits you and ignites your energy. The more affinity you feel with your cause, the more motivated you'll be to stick with it. This is the hardest part for most girls. Haven't you ever said to yourself, "I want to make a difference . . . but I don't know where to start?" Now's the time to figure that out.

You may want to review your "personal passion" list from Chapter 7 to get yourself excited. Afterwards, take out a fresh piece of paper or open to a page in your journal and create a new list: your ideal world.

YOUR IDEAL WORLD

A wonderful way to get ideas on how to help the world is to think about what your perfect vision of this Earth would be like. Make a list of things you'd want in this ideal world:

- ◉ How is it different from the world we currently live in?
- ◉ How do people interact and treat each other?

- How do you interact with others?
- What do your surroundings look like, physically?
- What is the biggest change that has taken place?

When you're done brainstorming, take a look at your list and pick one item that particularly compels you. Begin to contemplate how you could act on this issue to make a positive difference. What could you do right at this moment to help? How could you contribute in a long-term way? The more passionate you feel about your ideas, the better. It doesn't matter how big or small each idea is, since good deeds come in many sizes. Each deed is like a pebble cast into a pond, sending ripples infinitely in all directions. There are three major types of "ponds," all of them equally important:

1. The Home Pond: Service starts in the home, the place where we learned to share our first toy and resolve our conflicts over the TV remote control. From the moment we wake up until the moment our head hits the pillow each night, we make thousands of decisions about how we act and treat others. Do you listen with open ears as your little brother tells you about his day? Do you set the table for mom when you can tell she has had a hard time at work?

Bring the spirit of service into your home by taking advantage of the many opportunities you're given each day. Do something nice for all of your family members without expecting anything in return. Offer a free back massage, write a nice poem, or do the dishes without being asked. View your home as a laboratory of the spirit in which you can test recipes for love and service. Buddha once said, "Wherever you live is your temple, if you treat it like one."

2. The Community Pond: As soul searchers, we have a responsibility to give back to the places that educate, entertain, and watch us grow. The sense of belonging and security that comes from building community spirit lasts a lifetime. Many of us miss out on these rewards because we don't pay enough attention to our surroundings. In each community, there are signs of need and calls for help that must be answered. But first, we must listen.

What are the needs of your community? Does your school need help building a playground for the younger children? Could your elderly neighbor use someone to mow her lawn or shovel her snow? "Community is created and renewed when individuals act in love and serve each other," wrote Frederic and Mary Ann Brussat. We must constantly give back to our neighborhoods, schools, and congregations, because in finding our communities we find parts of ourselves.

3. The World Pond: The world . . . a pond? It may seem strange to imagine, but everything we do has an effect on the world at large. With the help of technology like the World Wide Web, our globe is becoming a smaller and smaller place, while our ability to change it is becoming greater and greater. As soul searching requires of us, we've got to figure out our unique contribution to the world. One way to do this is through volunteering.

How are you going to save the world? Don't run away from your lofty ambitions. Start a club, as described in Chapter 7. Organize a joint service effort, such as a charity drive for victims of floods, earthquakes, or famines. Pay attention to the needs of people all over the globe, from hungry children in Africa to female victims of violence around the world. Fight for universal causes: an end to sexism, racism, hunger, etc. We must take on our responsibility as citizens of the earth.

MORE SERVICE IDEAS

If you still need help thinking of ways to volunteer, here are a few more ideas to try. Ask parents, teachers, and friends if you need more ideas, or check out a book on volunteering (see Resources at the end of this chapter).

Start recycling, if you don't already. Reuse old containers, plastic bags, etc. Also, starting a compost heap is a great way to recycle food and create rich fertilizer.

Plan a neighborhood service project, such as a community trash walk. On a sunny weekend, rally together as many friends, neighbors, classmates, and family members as possible. Split up into pairs and walk around collecting litter. When everyone is done, gather back together and compare your bulging bags, basking in the feeling of accomplishment!

Real Teens Who've Made a Difference

Maybe you've heard stereotypical remarks about teenagers being troublemakers, but no one can deny the positive contributions we've made over the course of history. Here are a few stories of girls who set their minds on making a difference:

KORY JOHNSON

When Kory was nine, her older sister died. She investigated and discovered her neighborhood was a "cancer cluster" (a place where the number of people getting cancer is much higher than average). Determined to take action, the young girl formed Children for a Safe Environment (CSE) to encourage young people to speak out against environmental health hazards. More than 300 kids are now part of Kory's group, and they've won battles against many corrupt corporations that have tried to dump hazardous waste into poor neighborhoods. For her efforts, Kory won the 1998 Goldman Environmental Prize and a $125,000 scholarship, and the Ms. Foundation named her one of the Top 10 Role Models for 1999.

JENNIFER FLETCHER

Many schools in Jennifer's hometown had to get rid of art, music, dance, and drama classes because of budget cuts. The teenager was appalled and decided to stage a benefit concert to raise money to bring the arts back to the public schools. All on her own, she convinced rock star Jackson Browne to play, and raised close to $100,000. Next, she created ARTS ALIVE!, a nonprofit organization run by students, to distribute the money to the neediest schools. In 1999, Jennifer won the Seventeen magazine Volunteerism Award, which earned her a $10,000 college scholarship, $10,000 for ARTS ALIVE!, and dinner with First Lady Hillary Clinton.

CARLA DERRICK & LESLIE WILSON

These two friends used their own personal tragedies to help others. Carla lost an eye to cancer, and her friend Leslie lost a lung and a leg. Together they wrote, produced, and edited a video to answer questions for kids newly diagnosed with cancer. This video, called "How to Cope," helps hundreds of kids through a very difficult time. "Cancer changed my life," Carla said. "It was the hardest thing that I ever had to go through, and I made it, and I'm not afraid of anything now."

NICOLE MCLAREN

Nicole, who lives in Jamaica, was concerned about kids' lack of connection to world events and their feelings of helplessness in the face of global problems. So she created www.nation1.com, an Internet site for young people to discuss the world's problems. The site shows kids how to get involved with regional and global projects that interest them, find people with money to help fund their ideas, and hear the latest international news from kids in other countries. Companies like Swatch, Compaq, Apple, Motorola, and agencies like UNESCO (United Nations Educational, Scientific, and Cultural Organization) are financial supporters of Nicole's idea, giving money to Nation 1 to help it achieve its goals. The current project for Nation 1 and Nicole is recruiting 400 youth representatives to the next United Nations Assembly to inform world leaders about issues that are important to young people.

KRISTEN BELANGER

When she was nine, Kristen read about the rapid destruction of the rainforest in a Greenpeace magazine and immediately decided to get involved. Kristen and her friend Marcy designed a plan for a "Rainforest Day" at their elementary school, which they presented to their principal. With the help of classmates, they collected over $700 for their cause. Kristen didn't stop there. She started to hold clothing drives, and has collected over 2,300 pounds of warm clothing for those in need. Kristen's good deeds have given her a reason to feel good about herself, since she has "had the chance to change the lives of many people and make the world a little bit better."

Pay attention to politics. Call your members of Congress to let them know your beliefs, especially regarding issues that affect children or teens. Who else will stand up for us? Run for student government so that you can make a positive difference in your school.

Seek out volunteer organizations. Do some research on the various service groups in your community. Look in the phone book under "social service organizations" or "non-profit organizations" to find local groups in need of volunteers. Hospitals, homeless shelters, soup kitchens, literacy groups, environmental agencies, and childcare centers are great places to help out.

Adopt a grandparent. Many nursing homes have programs through which you can be paired with an elderly person of similar interests. If you keep in touch with your new "grandpa" or "grandma" by visiting and writing letters, you'll not only cheer him or her up, but you'll also have a new friend who's older and wiser than most!

Help out on holidays. If you ever get the feeling that holidays have been taken over by a materialistic, "Gimme presents!" attitude, add a deeper meaning to your celebration by serving others. For Thanksgiving, you can deliver food baskets to less fortunate families. For Halloween, you can make costumes for kids who can't afford them, or you can give some of your candy to kids in the hospital who can't go trick-or-treating. The next time a holiday comes along, don't let this great opportunity for giving pass you by.

Volunteer abroad. Next summer, while the rest of your friends go off to the beach or summer camp, consider going on a service vacation! This type of trip, usually organized by international volunteer programs, offers us the chance to travel to new places, work hard, and make the world a better place. It also teaches us to take risks and learn about different cultures and ways of life. The Internet is a great place to find out about this type of opportunity.

One summer I went as a volunteer to a Cuban community center. At first I didn't think I'd be able to stand the heat, bugs, lumpy mattresses and unfamiliar foods. But the trip forced me to reach within myself and see how much I was capable of doing without the help of my family or friends. I made lots of new friends, helped organize a long-neglected library, and showed myself how strong I really am. By spending your vacation time building houses, working in a health clinic, or doing some type of service in a foreign place, you can get in touch with your inner strength and courage and learn about another culture at the same time!

Join an environmental group, such as Friends of the Earth or the Environmental Defense Fund. These groups have vast amounts of resources and can show you how to make an impact on the world through all sorts of actions, big and small. Many teens feel that reconnecting with Mother Earth and fighting for her protection is a very important part of the soul searching journey.

Fight world hunger. According to UNICEF (United Nations Children's Fund), more than 600 million children around the globe go hungry each day. There are lots of ways you can fight hunger, especially if you're willing to educate yourself on the topic. Read as much as you can or support and volunteer for an organization like UNICEF or the Hunger Project. Then, take action! Raise money, write articles for the local newspaper, hold a Hunger Awareness Week at school. With your parent's permission, try fasting for a day and experience hunger for yourself. Really struggle to understand the suffering of hungry people around the world. Let them into your heart. This role-playing technique (putting yourself in the other person's shoes) works well with all kinds of activism. When you feel empathy strongly enough, you'll be ready to change the world. Go for it!

VOLUNTEER DAY

Several times a year, millions of people all across the country (and even the world) get together in an effort to make a difference. Here are some special volunteering dates to mark on your calendar:

April 22—Earth Day
This the most widely recognized national service day, a rare moment in which Americans take the time to plant trees, clean up streets, conserve energy, and pay attention to Mother Earth. What can *you* do?

Third Tuesday in April—National Youth Service Day

In 1997, over two million young people took part in this day to recognize and celebrate youth volunteer work. Organized by Youth Service America, this event has inspired over ten million hours of volunteer service and is the largest volunteer event in the world. Go to its website at www.servenet.org or call at (202) 296-2992 for information.

Fourth Saturday of October—Make a Difference Day

Started by the Points of Light Foundation, in collaboration with *USA Weekend,* Make a Difference Day reminds us of the tremendous impact we can have when we devote our time and energy to helping others. For more information, call (800) 416-3824.

THE DOS AND DON'TS OF SUCCESSFUL VOLUNTEERING

Volunteering isn't always easy. Sometimes it means waking up early or sacrificing time that could be spent playing soccer or hanging out with your friends. Even when you're trying hard to help, things won't always go your way. Sometimes people you're trying to help may get angered or embarrassed by your attention. Be prepared for some rejection, hard days, and self-sacrifice. But in the long run, I guarantee you that you'll be glad you did it.

DO have a flexible and open mind. Allow for some spontaneity—if things don't seem to be working one way, look for another solution.

DON'T get discouraged. Things aren't always perfect: you miss the bus, you let someone down, you feel uninspired. Stay with it, even when things look bleak.

DO make sure you're ready for whatever commitments you make. People are depending on you! For certain volunteer work, such as operating an advice hotline, training classes are offered. The more prepared you are, the more reliable and helpful you will be.

DON'T expect to change the world right away. If you're helping at an organization, you'll probably start out at the very bottom and have to work your way up. The more responsible you prove yourself to be, the faster this will happen.

DO celebrate your successes. Give yourself a pat on the back or an ice cream sundae when things go well. Enjoy the volunteering experience. And make sure you like what you're doing, or you won't stick with it.

BECOME THE SEA OF GALILEE

As soul searchers, we each must figure out our own special way of giving to the world. I must find my own way, and you must find yours. But no matter how you choose to give of your time, your love, and your spirit, remember the law of karma and the Sea of Galilee. The more we give, the more we receive. The more generous we are, the more our souls will be filled to overflowing.

"Service is the rent each of us pays for living—the very purpose of life," said Marian Wright Edelman, a children's advocate and civil rights activist. However you do it, choose today to become a citizen of the Earth in the best way you can, by giving back. As soul searchers, we are responsible for keeping our good karma replenished all the time.

What do YOU think?

Volunteering makes you feel good on the inside, knowing you've helped others because they needed it. The fact that you're putting others first is the coolest feeling.
—KATIE HEDBERG, AGE 14

I volunteer at day camps and in schools. I feel that volunteering opens the doors to personal growth and extends the horizons of how far a person can go.
—RIVKY THALER, AGE 17

I do a lot of volunteering. I find that it makes me very happy that I'm helping my community. I feel like I'm more a part of the town and considered an important person.
—RACHAEL BENTSEN, AGE 15

I've volunteered at a teen crisis hotline, a homeless shelter, and I'm currently volunteering at my community's wildlife shelter. All of the experiences have been completely different but have left me feeling great about myself because I know I've improved someone's life. Volunteering is a gift. I give my time to people I don't know, and, in return, they give me their gratitude.
—GREER JOHNSON, AGE 17

I teach piano lessons to underprivileged children. Watching them learn music and seeing the look in their eyes when they finally play a piece is an amazing thrill.
—CAITLIN DWYER, AGE 16

RESOURCES

The Kid's Guide to Service Projects: Over 500 Service Ideas for Young People Who Want to Make a Difference, by Barbara Lewis

A Student's Guide to Volunteering, by Theresa Foy DiGeronimo

Youth Service America
(202) 296-2992
www.servenet.org

Impact Online (matches volunteers with volunteer groups)
www.impactonline.org

CHAPTER 9

Become A Philosopher

CONSIDERING THE BIG QUESTIONS

When we're born, many things have already been decided for us: our sex, our nationality, our family, our race, etc. From that moment on, however, our lives enter a sequence of endless possibilities. We are responsible for deciding how to think, what to believe, and how to handle each opportunity that comes our way. "We invent ourselves out of ingredients we didn't choose, by a process we can't control," explains poet Lew Welch. "It is also possible to uninvent yourself."

But how do we begin "uninventing" ourselves and figuring out, from scratch, who we really are? Philosophy is the perfect vehicle for this, since it urges us to inspect and scrutinize our lives and our beliefs. Where do we come from and where are we going? By asking questions, we determine which viewpoints are truly our own, and which are the result of other people's urgings or expectations. As soul searchers, we can never accept prepackaged, one-size-fits-all truths.

Officially, most of us hold a mental picture of philosophy as a profession for ancient Greek men or brooding intellectuals. You're probably familiar with some of history's great truth-seekers, like Plato or Locke; maybe you've even studied them in school. What you may not realize is that *anyone* can be a philosopher in the most genuine sense of the word. Philosophy is not just a profession; it is also a way of thinking. The word philosopher means "lover of wisdom," and thus the only real criteria is that we embark upon a lifelong search for meaning and truth.

THE GREAT PHILOSOPHIES

To help us on our quest, it is often useful to study the advice of famous thinkers who've shaped the past. It's unlikely that you'll agree with every philosophy I'm about to present. But it's more fun that way, as long as you don't settle for mere disagreement. Press yourself further. Ask why. Find the benefits and limitations of each school of thought. Sift through the philosophies until you find a grain of truth in each to cherish.

The Natural Philosophers

What They Thought: In ancient Greece, around 460 B.C., the world's earliest certified philosophers began casting doubt upon traditional systems of belief. At the time, divine intervention was used as an excuse for almost everything that came about. Why did it rain? The gods were happy, of course. Why did people get sick? The gods were angry, obviously. Why did we lose the war? Surely, the gods were feeling vengeful.

These answers didn't satisfy a small group of Greeks, who came to be known as the *natural philosophers*. They decided to swim against the current, looking for better, more accurate ways of justifying curious phenomena like weather patterns and illness. By examining the physical world in search of explanations, these great thinkers uncovered many of nature's secrets and made great leaps in science and medicine. THEY TURNED THE TABLES ON POPULAR OPINION and awakened the masses to the need for logical inquiry.

What's the Point? Sometimes we forget that the majority isn't always right. Although it's now common knowledge that rain comes from condensed water vapors in the air, and sickness is a result of invading germs, most of us wouldn't have known better 2,000 years ago. . . and what if we had? How would we have acted if we'd known the truth behind rain or diseases, but no one else did?

Furthermore, what would we have done if we were alive during times of slavery? Or the Holocaust? Or the Salem witch hunts? What would we have done then? Let's take the example of the natural philosophers as a call for action in our own lives. We must never be afraid to question the norm and probe for deeper truths. In fact, why not banish the word "normal" from our vocabulary entirely? The only purpose of such a concept is to confine us, to limit our possibilities, and to make us fear our own eccentricities. The next time you're ridiculed for doing something zany, whether it's singing Michael Jackson songs in the shower, dancing alone at a party, or otherwise being 100 percent yourself, just smile and keep going. And if you feel like something's not fair among your friends, your family, your community, your country, or even your universe, stand up and do something about it, like a true natural philosopher.

Socrates

What He Thought: Sometimes said to be the most brilliant man in history, Socrates was always one (or two, or three) steps ahead of the rest of Athens, where he lived from 470-399 B.C. Despite his vast knowledge, Socrates never boasted of such wisdom. In fact, he often proclaimed, "One thing only I know, and that is that I know nothing." Tragically, many Greeks were distrustful of his quizzical demeanor, and a jury of 500 sentenced Socrates to death for crimes of "corrupting the youth" and "introducing new gods." In spite of this, he left a colossal imprint on the world, as the modern recognition of his name attests.

One of Socrates' essential contributions to society was his style of teaching, now know as the "Socratic method." After careful observation of his students, he realized that often, WHEN WE ASK A QUESTION OF ANOTHER PERSON, WE ALREADY KNOW THE ANSWER SOMEWHERE INSIDE OURSELVES. We merely need someone to guide us back to it. Socrates fervently believed that true understanding comes from within, and he refused to lecture or preach to his students; he questioned, debated, and discussed with them instead.

What's the Point? We can use the Socratic method in our own daily lives to help us break down stereotypes or reveal flaws in previous assumptions—here's how:

1. Begin with a statement or stereotype that's considered common knowledge. *Women must be physically attractive in order to be successful,* for example.

2. Now, turn the statement around and imagine that it's false. Search for any and every situation in which the statement is incorrect. *Could a woman be successful without being beautiful. . . or could she be beautiful without*

being physically attractive? Do I know any successful girls or women who aren't considered outwardly beautiful?

3. If you find an exception, you've discovered that your original assumption is false or imprecise. *Rosie O'Donnell has achieved great success without fitting the traditional standards of beauty. I consider Eleanor Roosevelt to be beautiful although she was not physically attractive by conventional measurements.*

4. Now that you've exposed the inaccuracy of your initial statement, you must rewrite it, taking any exceptions into account. *Although females are generally told they must be physically attractive in order to be successful, many accomplished women, like Rosie O'Donnell and Eleanor Roosevelt, have achieved great success without conforming to this standard of appearance.*

5. Return to Step 2 and test your revised statement, searching once again for exceptions. Repeat Steps 2 through 4 until you've created a statement that reveals the truth as accurately as possible.

Aristotle

What He Thought: Aristotle, who lived from 384-322 B.C., came from Greece and studied philosophy intensely from the age of seventeen. He came up with many theories about science, politics, mathematics, and life. Aristotle believed that "the whole is more than the sum of the parts," suggesting that THE INDIVIDUAL COMPONENTS OF A SITUATION ARE NOT AS IMPORTANT AS ITS OVERALL SIGNIFICANCE AND MEANING. If people started to consider how their actions affect the universe as a "greater whole," we'd probably have a lot less pollution, crime, and injustice in our society. Aristotle believed in the existence of three conditions required for happiness. In order for a person to find genuine fulfillment, all of these criteria must be met:

1. A life of pleasure and enjoyment

2. A life as a free and responsible citizen

3. A life as a thinker and philosopher

What's the Point? Aristotle also believed that moderation was the secret to inner contentment. Leading a life of balance means avoiding extremes, like eating too much or too little, working too hard in school or not enough, being too indulgent or not treating yourself to enough delights.

Do you agree with Aristotle's three requirements for happiness? Do you think it's possible to find joy without them? Do you possess these conditions in your own life? Think for a moment about what it means to be happy, then make your own list of criteria. Do you possess them all? If not, what's holding you back? Do you live a life of moderation? Do you or anyone else you know do things to the extreme? How does that affect you and them?

Descartes

What He Thought: Descartes is often called the father of modern philosophy, even though he was born more than 400 years ago. Similar to Socrates, he would begin examining a problem under the assumption that everything he already knew about it was false. He believed that WE MUST RID OURSELVES OF ALL OUR PRECONCEPTIONS AND PREJUDICES AND BUILD OUR OPINIONS FROM THE GROUND UP.

Not only did Descartes doubt past knowledge, he also felt unsure of his sensory perceptions. Isn't it possible that our senses deceive us? For example, in our sleep each night, we feel like we're really experiencing reality as we dream. I once had a dream in which I was pregnant, and that was probably the most fear I've ever felt in my life! As Descartes pointed out, "When I consider this carefully, I find not a single property which with certainty separates the waking state from the dream. How can you be certain that your whole life is not a dream?"

What's the Point? The separation between dreams and reality deeply puzzled Descartes. Eventually, he decided that since he doubted everything, he could at least be sure of one thing: that he doubted. A doubt is a thought, and someone must think a thought in order for it to exist. Thus, Descartes certified his existence by saying, "I think, therefore I am."

This observation is just as important for girls today as it was for Descartes in the 1600s. In order for us to truly feel alive, we must be thoughtful, reflective human beings. I often find myself so wrapped up in school and sports that I start living on autopilot. In a zombie-like state, I do my homework, listen to my teachers, memorize vocabulary words . . . all to be forgotten the next day! I learn so much more effectively when I'm really exercising my brain and mulling things over inside my head.

Ask yourself how alive you really are. Have you ever felt like you're living inside a dream, or maybe even inside the body of a robot!? Do you work hard in school for the sake of getting good grades or pleasing your parents, instead of seeking wisdom for yourself? Do you memorize the dates of the Renaissance or World War I just long enough to write them on your history test, and then forget them again? Make a pledge to utilize your brain's true potential from this day forward. Repeat to yourself each morning the words of Descartes, "I am; I exist—that is certain. But for how long? For as long as I am thinking."

Immanuel Kant

What He Thought: During the Enlightenment movement of the eighteenth century, Immanuel Kant developed many theories on the nature of human perception. He decided that WE CAN NEVER KNOW FOR CERTAIN WHAT THE WORLD IS LIKE IN ITSELF; WE CAN ONLY KNOW WHAT IT IS LIKE AS IT APPEARS TO US. What the world is like *for you* is only one possible reality.

If you've ever worn a pair of rose-tinted glasses, you probably see what Kant meant. When you put the glasses on, everything in the room suddenly becomes a shade of pink or red. If you didn't know better, wouldn't you be tempted to declare that the whole world is red? Fortunately, your brain is sophisticated enough to realize that the new color of the objects is a direct result of the glasses you are wearing—not a genuine attribute of the world around you.

What's the Point? Kant believed that we all approach the world wearing our own unique pair of "glasses." Everything we see is first filtered through the lenses, preventing us from understanding the pure and absolute truth. Our past experiences influence our present perceptions in powerful ways. To give you an unpleasant example, I once ate a lot of popcorn at the movies. The next morning, I came down with a virus and had an upset stomach all day. From that moment on, popcorn stopped being my favorite snack and became a food

I wouldn't touch with a ten-foot pole. Of course, the actual taste of popcorn hadn't changed; my mentality had. It took me an entire year to get over it.

In our daily attempts to communicate with others, it's important to remember that we each have our own ways of seeing things. The next time someone hurts your feelings or makes you angry, envision looking through her "glasses" or walking in her shoes. Really use your imagination. When I went out to lunch and my waitress was really late with my meal, I started to get quite annoyed. *She doesn't even deserve a tip*, I found myself thinking bitterly, until I remembered Kant's philosophy. It dawned on me as I saw her rush from table to table balancing plates of food on her forearm: being a waitress is exhausting. As the dark bags under her eyes attested, she'd probably been working long hours, darting from one customer to the next with as much graciousness as she could muster. After this mental exercise, I was perfectly content waiting for my sandwich, and I even gave my waitress a friendly smile when it finally arrived!

The Existentialists

What They Thought: Human freedom was the obsession of the Existentialist philosophers who lived around the beginning of the twentieth century. They made the daring proclamation that there is no singular right and wrong; each person should design his or her own code of morality. WE OUGHT TO FIND A UNIQUE PURPOSE AND WAY OF LIVING, INSTEAD OF LEANING ON THE CRUTCH OF SOCIETY'S DEMANDS.

Have you ever assumed that you'll inevitably go to college, find a well-paying job, get married, and have children, simply because all of this is expected of you? Well, the existentialists argue that you should follow the path in life that makes you happiest, regardless of what others think. "I must find a truth that is true for me . . . the idea for which I can live or die," stated Soren Kierkegaard, one of the first existentialists.

What's the Point? By now, you've hopefully figured out that soul-searching is the quest for *personal* meaning, not for some goal others have set. It's easier said than done, however! One way to help us practice this existentialist principle is to make a chart of other people's expectations. Grab a piece of paper and draw a line down the middle. On one side of the page, list the various individuals who have influenced your life: parents, siblings, teachers, coaches, grandparents, friends, etc. On the other side, list what each of these people seems to expect from you, either explicitly or indirectly. Does your dad want you to be an athletic superstar? Does your mom intend for you to love politics, just like she always has?

When you're done writing, look over your list carefully. You may notice some contradicting messages—like if you're expected to be a stellar student who spends all her time studying, while also participating in tons of clubs, sports, and social activities. Surely, that's too much for any girl to balance. Comb your list for any expectations you just can't meet (or don't want to meet). Now that you've pinpointed them, you can decide to accept them or reject them. You may even want to discuss your list with your parents, friends, coaches, or other people on it, if that's not too difficult. Remember that this life is your own, not anyone else's.

The Feminists

What They Thought (and still think!): Philosophy was traditionally a man's domain until the feminist movement shook things up a bit. Although feminists can be found at many points on the belief spectrum and through many eras of time, all have been unified by a common cause: LIBERATION AND EQUALITY FOR THE FEMALE SEX. Back in 1792, a philosopher named Mary Wollstonecraft defended women's right to education. Then, in the mid-1800s, a group of bold women including Elizabeth Cady Stanton and Susan B. Anthony began fighting for women's suffrage (the right to vote, which they didn't win until 1920). In the 1960s, the hippie generation reawakened feminism, hoping to achieve economic justice, reproductive freedom, political representation, and equal opportunities across the board.

Yet true feminism ventures beyond these political and tangible objectives, striking at a more philosophical core. According to author and activist Robin Morgan, "The feminist vision has always been about love—not a Hallmark card sentimentalized, cheapened imitation, but the wild, furious, enraged, cleansing, energetic love that demands change. . ." Seeking equality means more than just winning the right to wear pants or vote in presidential elections. It means being able to love our bodies, our minds, and our lives in all ways possible, in each hour of each day.

What's the Point? It should be pretty obvious that feminism has an impact on our lives as girls and future women. Every soul searching girl wants to be treated with respect and given equal opportunities. So how can we be feminists in our own right? First of all, we've got to learn our *herstory*. This means reading up on the many fascinating and influential women that are overlooked in textbooks, but deserve our attention nevertheless. Find role models among great names like Marie Curie, Simone de Beauvoir, Harriet Tubman, Mother Jones, and Zora Neale Hurston. Then, stand up for our sex, even in small ways. Last year, when my soccer coach told us that we could do "girl" push-ups (modified, easier ones) instead of "real" push-ups, I told him why I didn't like his terminology. Whenever you have an opportunity to share your feminist values, grab it. Change doesn't occur overnight, but it does come with hard work and faith.

WHAT'S YOUR PHILOSOPHY?

Okay, so now you've been introduced to some of history's important philosophical movements. You've heard other people's thoughts on truth, beauty, equality, and freedom. But the important question remains: What do *you* think? What's *your* philosophy? Before your brain gets too exhausted, I want to share a few more exercises that might help you figure it out.

Imagine Your Funeral. Yes, I certainly realize how creepy and bizarre this suggestion might seem. Imagining your own funeral can be a strange or even painful idea, depending on your past experiences. Even so, to consider death means to consider life. Many psychologists use this visualization technique as a wake-up call to help their clients reflect on their priorities while they still have a chance to change them.

When you're ready, take a trip to your own funeral. Think for a moment about your regrets. Are you pleased with the way you treated others? What about the way you treated yourself? Walk around the room and listen to what people are saying. What special attributes of yours are they eulogizing? Is it what you hoped for? Find the newspaper and read your obituary. How do you feel about its content? When you're ready, come back to reality and think about what you've learned. Let your discoveries be inspirational, not depressing. As

What do YOU think?

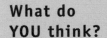

I like to think that my philosophy and spiritual beliefs can serve as a backbone for when I have to make moral decisions. I think that my beliefs make it so I have a more open perspective on the world. My philosophies and beliefs can also be a comfort to me when I'm feeling down or doubting myself.

—JULIA HALPRIN JACKSON, AGE 16

I guess you could also say that I'm a humanist. I believe that we are a miracle, and the fact that we're here by chance is a testament to the humor and wonder of the universe. That the art of Michelangelo and Bach and Shakespeare could spring from human minds thrills me, and makes me wonder what else we're capable of.

—CAITLIN DWYER, AGE 16

a young woman with your entire life stretched out before you, you've got plenty of chances to seize the day.

Invent the Anti-You. In figuring out who we are, it can be surprisingly helpful to figure out who we are *not*. In your head, create a character that is the absolute opposite of you. Think about how she (or he? or it?) looks, sounds, and acts. Imagine a day in which she mingles with your family, talks to your teachers, and has a sleep-over with your friends. What is her day like? Why is she so different from you?

When you're done, reflect on this new character you've created. Maybe even write a story about her or draw a picture. Your feelings about the Anti-You can shed light upon the traits you possess, both positive and negative. For example, I noticed that the Anti-Me listened very carefully whenever people spoke to her, instead of focusing on her own preoccupations. I took this as a hint that I should perk up my ears and learn to be more receptive. Seek whatever knowledge your Anti-You has to impart.

Skeletons in the Closet. One of the most revealing things about us all, as I'm sure you know, is the secrets we keep. The things we hide can teach us a lot about who we are. Spend a moment thinking about your deepest secrets. Maybe you've done or said something that would be too mortifying to disclose. Or it's possible that your most classified information isn't an experience, but rather a thought, feeling, or dream you've had. I often considered how horrifying it would be if someone invented a machine that could read minds; we'd all probably hide away in the basement forever!

Since we can't escape from our own secrets, we might as well use them as tools for growth. Reflect upon how your secrets shape you as a human being. Why do you hide the things you do? What makes your secrets so mortifying (or uninteresting!)? Do you have any secrets from *yourself*? Take some time to open the closet of skeletons and dust things off. Who knows what you'll find in there?

JUST THINK

Don't get too compulsive about mastering your philosophy and becoming the next Socrates. Every once in a while, give yourself some time to think about whatever's on your mind, even if it lacks sophistication. You can think about something that's bothering you. You can think about the things you love. You can think about relationships, or clouds, or lemonade, or yesterday, or tomorrow. After my cat has been indoors for too many days in a row, we always let her outside for a few hours to romp around and enjoy herself. Our minds deserve a similar chance to frolic.

RESOURCES

The Book of Questions, by Gregory Stock (a great book full of philosophical questions to ponder alone or with friends)

The Anatomy of Freedom: Feminism in Four Dimensions, by Robin Morgan

The Complete Idiot's Guide to Philosophy, by Jay Stevenson, Ph.D.

Girls Who Rocked the World 1 & 2, by Amelie Welden and Michelle Roehm

Herstory: Women Who Changed the World, edited by Ruth Ashby and Deborah Gore Ohrn

The 100 Most Influential Women of All Time, by Deborah Felder

Sophie's World: A Novel About the History of Philosophy, by Jostein Gaardner

101 Philosophy Problems, by Martin Cohen

The Story of Philosophy: The Lives and Opinions of the World's Greatest Philosophers from Plato to John Dewey, by Will Durant

Visit these websites for more information on women philosophers:
www.womeninworldhistory.com
www.greatwomen.org

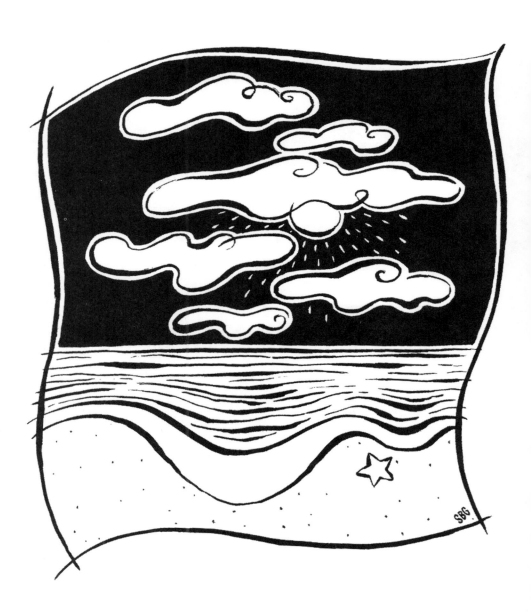

CHAPTER 10

Explore World Religions

IS THERE A BUDDHA IN YOU?

Religion. . .we've all heard the word but what exactly does it mean? Is it church? God? Heaven? According to the dictionary, religion is "a belief in and reverence for a supernatural power recognized as the creator and governor of the universe." Ever since the beginnings of recorded time, religion has been one of the most powerful forces of society. People have lived and died for their spiritual beliefs. Wars have been started for the sake of religion, and peace has sprung from its depths as well. Humans have worshiped everything imaginable, from the sun and the moon, to the forces of wind and fire, to spiritual leaders like Mohammed, Buddha, and Jesus Christ.

Religion can also be one of the most compelling tools available to us on our soul searching quests. It helps us make sense of difficult questions like, "Why am I here?" and "What is my purpose in life?" Through religion, we can better understand our place in the world and learn how to live more purposefully. It is, in many respects, our spiritual compass.

What role has religion played in your life up until now? Some girls grow up against a backdrop of strong pious traditions, while others are born into families in which both parents belong to different denominations, or no denomination at all. Most of us tend to adhere to the religion of our parents, but some girls choose to venture on their own spiritual paths.

I'm not here to advocate any particular faith, but I do think it's important to have a defined set of religious beliefs—even if that means not believing in God. You may choose to belong to an organized, structured religion, such as

Christianity or Judaism, in which you go to regular religious services and adhere to a certain set of moral expectations. This type of spiritual community can be a wonderful source of comfort and joy, as well as a place to turn for advice and insight. On the other hand, you may choose to form your own set of sacred beliefs, separate from the rules of a church or synagogue. This approach has its benefits, too; you can draw from various religious and spiritual teachings to help you find a unique method of worship.

EXPLORING CHOICES

If you ever decide to buy a car, you'll probably shop around, compare prices, take a few test drives, and think long and hard before making a purchase. You won't just immediately buy the first car they show you, right? And you won't just buy the same car your parents drive without thinking twice, right? Well, the same should be true of your religious beliefs, considering that spirituality is more essential than a car could ever hope to be. In order to understand religion's value most effectively, it's best to examine it from all points of view. With each faith we explore, even the ones we do not accept as our own, we become better acquainted with various ways of seeing the world, God, and ourselves. We learn to appreciate and respect other cultures and ways of life, regardless of whether we agree with them. This tolerance helps us embrace the wisdom of other traditions without relinquishing the integrity of our own beliefs.

RELIGIONS OF THE WORLD

To help us begin our exploration, the following is a brief description of some of the world's major religions and what we can learn from them. Many of the religions you're probably familiar with, while others might be new to you. You certainly aren't expected to agree with all of them, of course, but practice keeping an open mind. Look for the grains of truth within each culture and each belief system. Along with the basic descriptions of each religion is a glimpse of what's special or unique about it, followed by a pearl of wisdom to be found in it that we can carry on our soul searching journeys.

Christianity

The Basics: The most widely-practiced religion in the United States, Christianity is based around the life, death, and resurrection of Jesus Christ some 2,000 years ago. Followers of Christianity read the Bible and accept Jesus as the Son of God, who died for the sins of the world. When it comes to the issue of death, the soul is believed to be immortal, and it passes on into the glorious Kingdom of Heaven.

What's Special: An interesting thing about the Christian faith is the diversity of ways in which it is practiced. There are many communities of Christianity, including Catholics, Seventh-Day Adventists, Pentecostals, Baptists, Mormons, Christian Scientists, Unitarians, and Amish, to name just a few; each has its own unique ways of honoring God! For example, the Amish people seek to emulate the life of Jesus Christ as closely as possible, which entails dressing in simple, unadorned outfits and shunning the use of modern technology and even electricity. Roman Catholics follow the guidance of their spiritual leader in Rome, the Pope. Christian Scientists believe that our bodies can be healed by faith in God alone; they refuse to use common medicines that the average person might take for a cough or cold, turning to prayer instead. Mormons believe that God continues to give revelation to a modern prophet and each person can receive their own inspiration and guidance from God.

A Pearl of Christian Wisdom: FAITH

The New Testament of the Bible is full of brilliant parables in which Jesus reveals many truths about the world around us. One example, the parable of the mustard seed, offers quite relevant advice to soul searchers. In the story, Jesus reminds us how puny and weak the mustard seed appears at first glance. It is smaller than most of the other seeds on earth. However, when planted, it grows up and becomes greater than all the herbs around it. The mustard seed shoots up into a great tree, "so that the birds of the air come and nest in its branches."

The mustard seed, said Jesus, can be compared to the Kingdom of Heaven. Our faith and spirituality may seem puny and weak at first, and would probably appear unimpressive to the casual passerby who didn't know much about nurturing or faith. However, as we come to better understand ourselves and trust in a higher power, we begin to expand in unexpected and amazing ways. Like the mustard tree, we eventually grow so much that our spirituality encompasses more than our own confined space—it reaches out to others much like the tree provides shelter for the birds. Whenever we get discouraged with our soul searching progress, we can have faith in Jesus' reminder that all great trees were once tiny seeds.

Judaism

The Basics: The religion we now call Judaism began in Palestine over 4,000 years ago. The Jewish faith is one of very strong historical roots, stretching back to Abraham—the first man to enter into a covenant with God. In the Hebrew Bible (the Torah), the lineage and covenant of the Israelite people are followed through a series of prophets such as Isaac, Joseph, and Moses. Jews are monotheistic (believing in *one* all-powerful deity), and consider themselves God's chosen people who find protection and salvation in their faith.

What's Special: Judaism has given birth to many aspects of modern society. From its roots sprung two of the world's largest religions, Christianity and Islam. The Jewish faith also brought us the Ten Commandments, a very important set of moral guidelines that have led millions of people for centuries. According to the Torah, God delivered the Ten Commandments to the prophet Moses, who then brought them to the Israelites at the foot of Mount Sinai. Inscribed upon two tablets were rules such as "Thou shall not take the Lord's name in vain. . . Thou shall not murder . . . Thou shall not steal. . ." These ten rules for life, which you've probably heard before, offer very clear expectations about how people are meant to conduct their lives.

❦ A Pearl of Jewish Wisdom: REFLECTION

Judaism puts great emphasis on taking time to ask questions and reflect. "Judaism perceives a certain stillness, an almost indescribable placidity and perfection that we can sometimes glimpse behind the turmoil of the world," says Rabbi David A. Wolpe. But first, he believes, we must be ready for it. "It's not something that we can see or hear, but it can be felt."

In order to prepare for such a task, people of the Jewish faith believe in observing the Sabbath, a day of rest and spiritual observation. On this day, work and chores are replaced by relaxation, introspection, and enjoyment of life. Even if you're not Jewish, you can observe your own version of the Sabbath by taking time each weekend to listen to your favorite music, go for a walk with your family, reflect on your spiritual principles, and delight in being alive.

Islam

The Basics: The Islamic faith teaches that the world has seen many important prophets, including Abraham, Moses, and Jesus. But the last prophet was named Mohammed and he is believed to have received messages from God over 1,400 years ago. Islam now has more than one billion followers, known as Muslims, throughout the world. Muslims assert their faith in God, called Allah, by following His revelations as written in the Koran.

What's Special: Islam encourages its believers to help their fellow man and also to make a pilgrimage to the holy city of Mecca (in Saudi Arabia) before they die. During the sacred month of Ramadan (the ninth month of the Muslim calendar, beginning in December and ending in January), they must fast from sunrise to sunset. Muslims also pledge to uphold ideals of honesty, charity, and devotion. These teachings, thoroughly outlined in the Koran, are reinforced in places of daily worship called mosques.

A Pearl of Islamic Wisdom: PRAYER

From a very early age, followers of Islam are taught to seek guidance and serenity through the act of prayer. Muslims traditionally pray five times a day, facing Mecca. It is a method of communicating with a Higher Power, of looking *inward* by reaching *upward*.

Many of us are well-acquainted with superficial prayers of desire. *(Oh, dear God, please don't let me flunk this math test!)* But what about more rewarding types of prayer? As we grow older and seek independence, we often forget how soothing it is to rely on something or someone greater than ourselves. Using prayer, we can release our fears, express our gratitude, and share our joys. We are never alone. Muslims make an entire ritual of prayer, beginning with a ceremony of changing into clean dress, washing themselves, and laying out a prayer rug in the direction of Mecca. They use ritual movement during their prayers, to unite body and soul. The next time you feel discomfort or anguish stirring in your soul, create your own ritual to call upon Allah, Jesus, Brahman, Kindness, or whatever else you may believe in, asking for guidance.

Buddhism

The Basics: More than 2,500 years ago, a prince was born in India by the name of Siddhartha Gautama. Determined to achieve liberation from suffering, Siddhartha left his life of luxury and began searching for wisdom. After a long and difficult quest, he finally reached Nirvana (enlightenment) while meditating beneath a fig tree. From that day forward, followers called him the Buddha, meaning "awakened one," and flocked from miles around to hear his teachings on principles such as compassion, inner peace, and liberation. The Buddha's writings have been translated into almost 5,000 pages of text and sixteen volumes. The first three volumes, called the *Middle Length Sayings,* contain the most essential of the Buddha's teachings.

What's Special: Unlike most religious founders, the Buddha himself made no claims to divine origin. He recognized that there have been many buddhas in the past and that there are many buddhas yet to come. In fact, every man and woman has the potential to become an "awakened one." Within each of us lies "Buddha Nature," an innate, underlying state of mind untouched by negative emotions or thoughts. Followers of Buddhism seek access to this Buddha Nature by following teachings such as the "Four Noble Truths" and the "Eightfold Path," which offer guidance on how to find liberation.

A Pearl of Buddhist Wisdom: MINDFULNESS
A very special part of the Buddhist tradition is the practice of living in the moment. To be mindful means to be acutely aware of every movement, every sensation, and every thought we have throughout the day. It involves living in the present tense, instead of in the past or future. The Buddha once said that life comes down to one thing—staying awake. He wasn't warning us from dozing off in class or telling us not to enjoy our slumber at night; the Buddha was teaching us *the beauty of the here and now.*

"The next time you have a tangerine to eat, please put it in the palm of your hand and look at it in a way that makes the tangerine real," instructs renowned

Buddhist teacher Thich Nhat Hanh. How can we make it real? A Buddhist might begin with the decision to eat *consciously*, instead of approaching her food absentmindedly like most of us tend to do. Then, after taking a seat at the kitchen table and placing the tangerine before her in a moment of examination, she would slowly begin to eat. As she did so, she would relish each detail of the tangerine on her tongue and thus experience the true pleasure of living in the moment. "Peeling the tangerine, smelling it, and tasting it, you can be very happy," reminds Thich Nhat Hanh. The next time you sit down to eat, make it a practice in mindfulness, and really try to experience your food. You'll be amazed to find that a simple tangerine can become a tool for spiritual enlightenment!

Hinduism

The Basics: Since its origination some 3,000 years ago in India, Hinduism has acquired over 700 million followers. Unlike most other popular religions of our time, Hinduism has no founder or fixed creed. Although Hindus believe in a central Creator, called Brahman, there exist many other Hindu gods such as Vishnu, the god of space and time, and Durga, the goddess of motherhood. Each god has a unique personality and symbolic purpose, as described in the sacred Hindu scriptures called the Vedas.

What's Special: People of the Hindu faith believe in the concept of reincarnation, which states that we have each lived many lives and are reborn again upon our death. We each consist of two parts: body and soul. The body is like an outward robe we cast away when we've outworn it, but our souls endure forever in a chain of rebirths. "The body is ruled by passion and desires and meaningless ambitions," explains religious expert Joseph Gaer. "But the soul is ruled by serenity and the tranquil search for truth." When this truth is finally realized, Hindus believe that we escape the tedious cycle of reincarnation and enter Nirvana (similar to the Buddhist belief).

A Pearl of Hindu Wisdom: FORGIVENESS

Like many other religious traditions, Hinduism teaches its followers about the power of reconciliation. "If you want to see the brave, look at those who can forgive," reads the sacred Hindu poem *The Bhagavad Gita*. "If you want to see the heroic, look at those who can love in return for hatred."

Surely, we all know how challenging it is to love our enemies, but releasing past negativity helps us move forward on our soul searching path. The Hindu approach to life makes this process easier by teaching its followers about the holiness inherent in each human being. When two Hindus greet each other, they bow slightly with their hands folded against their breastbones. This salutation is a gesture honoring the divinity inside each person, the glorious spirit we *all* possess within. When someone hurts our feelings or wrongs us in some way, we must take a moment to remember her inner splendor and honor it. With this, it becomes easier to release our bitterness and feel at peace within our own skin.

Shinto

The Basics: From the very beginnings of their culture, many Japanese people have worshiped the mysterious forces of nature in a religion called Shinto. Living in a country ruled by devastating typhoons, erupting volcanoes, and terrifying tsunamis, it's no surprise that the Japanese felt a humbling reverence toward the forces of nature. They named these forces "kami," and sought to honor them through prayer, sacrifice, and ritual.

What's Special: Shintoism is rarely practiced outside the borders of Japan, and its modern-day practitioners are often Buddhists or Christians simultaneously, since Shinto does not demand exclusivity. A profound love of nature, as seen in each blade of grass or sunrise, is required of its followers. To show their adoration, Shintoists have many temples in which they pray and bring offerings like food, origami art, or spears. With these rituals, they seek to make the heart of kami and their own hearts one undivided entity.

A Pearl of Shinto Wisdom: RESPECT FOR NATURE

Living in present-day America amidst skyscrapers and concrete sidewalks, it's easy to fall out of touch with the harmony of the natural world. By intimate contact with our environment, Japanese commentator Inazo Nitobe says that we can learn the "healing power in the flower and the grass, in the mountains and streams, in the rain and the clouds." Shintoism urges us to seek therapeutic healing in all that surrounds us.

Even those of us who live in crowded cities or suburbs can still relish the scent of a rosemary plant in our window, or the sight of a squirrel burying an acorn in the park. Many Shintoists rise early to admire the sunrise, and others find unique ways of worshiping kami by painting, singing, and writing poetry. "Why seek afar for the divine?" Mr. Nitobe asks us. "It is in the objects around you."

Hopis

The Basics: The Hopi are a Pueblo Indian people who live in northern Arizona and are still strongly connected to their religion and history. Unlike most modern faiths, Hopi religious practice has more to do with honoring cultural traditions than following some sort of hierarchical church organization or method of worship. An important part of the religion is the Kachina—the spirit essence of everything in the natural world. This essence encapsulates everything from rain to animals, sunlight to ashes, and is honored in special Kachina dances and carefully carved *tihu* dolls.

What's Special: As children, we all heard fairy tales like "The Tortoise and the Hare" that were meant to entertain us while conveying important moral lessons. Well, the Hopi people invest tremendous powers in these types of oral legends, and they often use storytelling to communicate their spiritual and religious teachings. Instead of directly stating various tribal beliefs, the Hopi ancestors encoded a variety of messages within their fables, which have been passed down for many generations.

A Pearl of Hopi Wisdom: PATIENCE
In the holy stories of the Southwest Hopis, there is a Divine Mother named Spider Woman. Why on Earth would the Hopis choose a spider to represent a sacred deity? Well, next time you get a chance, observe a spider in action and you'll surely understand. A spider can spend many hours weaving the most intricate and elegant home found on the planet. When her web is damaged or broken, she rebuilds each tiny strand with patience, bit by bit. She will not rest until her home is restored to its regal splendor, where she waits for dinner to find entrapment in the glistening threads.

The Hopis remind us that we have much to learn from the plants and animals around us. Did you ever imagine that within the home of a single spider we could find a metaphor for sacred life? As Edward Hays observes in his book *Pray All Ways*, "Like the spider, we must return again and again to rebuild our webs by bringing together the threads of our lives and uniting them to the divine center within." The next time the tasks before you seem endless or you're thinking, "I want it NOW!" remember the Holy Spider Woman and the great gift of patience.

Baha'i

The Basics: The Baha'i faith arose in 1844 out of Islamic tradition. It began when a prophet named Bab heralded the arrival of "One greater than Himself" who would bring great wisdom and unity to the Earth. Nineteen years later, a man named Baha'u'llah in Iran claimed to be this special person, and thus became leader of the Baha'i religion. Baha'i followers believe that there is only one God, the source of all Creation, and that this God is everlasting and unknowable.

What's Special: The Baha'i religion is unique because of its strong emphasis on unity. "The earth is but one country," declares a popular Baha'i saying, "and mankind its citizens." Followers believe that although God is unknowable, He sends many prophets to communicate His will. Moses, Buddha, Jesus, Mohammed, and Baha'u'llah are all examples of these messengers from God. Each of them carries a unique and important message that ought to be heard.

A Pearl of Baha'i Wisdom: TOLERANCE

By believing that all religions spring from the same spiritual source and have value in some way or another, Baha'is offer us a lesson in open-mindedness. To them, the many world religions are simply different paths up the same mountain. Holding tolerance close to their hearts as an important trait, the Baha'is have fought for equality among all races and sexes.

Many people confuse the concept of religious tolerance with indifference or naiveté. To be tolerant, we must value the right of each person to hold beliefs different from our own, even when we think those beliefs are incorrect. When we reach the most profound levels of tolerance, we cease to be threatened by foreign ideas; instead, we seek to find truth and wisdom in each new viewpoint we encounter. By approaching the world with arms outstretched, our souls become infused with the power of many peoples and beliefs.

The Search

As with philosophy, asking questions is an important part of any religious journey. In grappling with your own beliefs, you may find it helpful to consider some common spiritual questions:

- Do I believe in a God or Higher Power?
- If so, how do I relate to that God or Higher Power?
- What kinds of religious rituals are important in my life?
- Do I believe in heaven or hell?
- Is there an after-life?
- What is death?

Spiritual Stages

Another interesting thing to consider is the concept of religious stages. Experts in theology have discovered a traditional pattern of religious growth. Obviously, not all of us fit neatly into this pattern of six faith stages. While most of us move chronologically through the stages, with few people reaching the final ones, others of us remain perfectly content to stay in one particular stage throughout our lives, or to experience several stages simultaneously.

Stage 1: MAGIC
According to Rev. Scotty McLennan, in his book *Finding Your Religion*, the traditional faith stages begin with the Magic stage. In this period, which is experienced by young children, God is perceived as an all-powerful, magical, do-gooder. Upon their very first introduction to God, children tend to view Him in this mystical light, granting Him full responsibility for everything that happens in the world: good weather, car crashes, etc.

Stage 2: REALITY
Around the age of six, children generally begin to separate fact from fantasy,

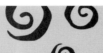

What do YOU think?

A Humanities class I took last year opened up my eyes to the many religions of the world. All of a sudden, I began to appreciate the traditions and rituals of Judaism, Taoism, Buddhism, Confucianism, and many other religions that had previously been foreign to me. This new knowledge got me thinking. Why don't I try to experience as many different religious services as I can? So one Sunday morning, my friend Sally and I decided to attend a Unitarian Universalist Church. The experience was completely new for both of us, and it helped us to learn how other people worship. We continue to attend various services, including going to a synagogue and a Catholic mass. Each new place of worship I attend adds to my beliefs and helps me create a clear sense of my spirituality.

—GREER JOHNSON, AGE 17

I am Christian, which is a very important part of my life. To me, God is loving, caring, and always looking after us to make sure we do our best. I'm always happy when I think of all the miracles in my life and everything good that has happened to me. He makes me who I am and helps me be a good person and to learn to love everyone, even though it is not easy.

—RACHAEL BENTSEN, AGE 15

marking their entrance into the Reality stage. During this period, God is seen more tangibly as a person. (Remember that image of an old man sitting in a throne with a long white beard?) God is thought to be influenced by promises, good deeds, and prayers, creating a cause-and-effect relationship between Him and His follower.

Stage 3: DEPENDENCE

During adolescence, there is often a great struggle between the next two stages: Dependence and Independence. In the Dependence stage, young people tend to feel a great longing for a personal relationship with God, in hopes of finding unconditional love and acceptance. They see God as similar to a parent figure, watching over them, protecting them, and possibly feeling anger or disappointment when they deviate from His governance.

Stage 4: INDEPENDENCE

The Independence stage, on the other hand, involves a disregard for institutions and strict traditions. "Instead of relying on outsiders, social conventions, and spiritual advisors to define one's religious orientation," explains Rev. McLennan, "the late teenager or young adult begins to find spiritual authority within. This is a common time for the individual to say, 'I'm spiritual, but not religious.'" It can often be hard to choose between having a close personal relationship with God, as in the Dependence stage, and having complete autonomy over your beliefs, as established in the Independence stage.

Stage 5: INTERDEPENDENCE

The final two stages are usually the domain of the older and wiser. The Interdependence stage involves the reconciliation of traditions and freedoms. It is a stage in which individuals once again appreciate the sacredness of religious symbols, sensing the spiritual richness to be found in them, without abandoning their more logical and analytical beliefs. Celebrating religious holidays or going through rituals such as Holy Communion can be spiritually nourishing, a truth which people in the Independence stage often neglect. On the other hand, people in the Dependence stage can be blinded by traditions and regulations. By combining the wisdom of these two stages, the Interdependence stage takes a person to new spiritual heights. And yet, in this stage you can experience some paradoxes: you might pray to God and envision Him or Her as a person while you understand that God is really not a human form.

What do YOU think?

Judaism is a way for me to experience tradition and feel connected to something larger than myself. Whenever life seems too overwhelming or stressful, I know I can turn to religion for peace of mind.
—ZOE WISEMAN, AGE 16

I don't believe in God, but I still have a spiritual side. I still believe in the therapy that spirituality brings, and I believe that when someone dies, their spirit lives on through other people. I am very unhappy when people think that I'm cursed by the devil for not believing in "God." I feel proud and confident in my beliefs; I respect others' right to believe differently. When tolerance, on either side, isn't used, it's very upsetting to me.
—ANONYMOUS

The closest philosophy to my own is probably the Buddha. His outlook was meant to cut straight to the heart, the essence of reality and our universe.
—CAITLIN DWYER, AGE 16

Stage 6: UNITY

In the final stage, Unity, all paradoxes melt away to reveal God in an "all-pervasive" way. God is seen in everything and everyone. At this spiritual peak, ego attachments dissolve and love becomes the dominant force in life. According to Rev. McLennan, people in this stage "possess a universalizing compassion and a vision of universal community beyond all forms of tribalism." For this reason, they are able to communicate in depth with people of all different faith stages and religions. People who attain this level of enlightenment tend to become revered and respected leaders of society, such as Gandhi, Mother Teresa, and the Dalai Lama.

When I first read about these stages, I was a bit confused. I felt myself to be in the "Independent" stage, yet I saw that various parts of me also existed in several other stages. Sometimes, while gazing at the stars on warm summer evenings, I sense God as all-pervasive and beautiful. Yet other times, when I'm faced with an incredibly hard task, I pray to God for help as if He or She were a parent figure.

Is it important to choose a label for my current stage? Absolutely not. There is no need for categorization, unless you find it helpful. It is also unnecessary to rush yourself along the "spirituality ladder," as I found myself tempted to do after reading about the stages. I figured, "Well, I guess I better move on to the next stage if I want to keep making progress!" Each stage is valid and important in its own way, and life shouldn't be seen as a race up the spiritual mountain. Enjoy the journey and learn from each stage.

WHAT'S THE POINT?

Religion has something different to offer each of us, regardless of our particular "stage" or set of beliefs. It can add hope, guidance, and a *sense of purpose* to your life. Of course, you may decide that religion doesn't suit your particular state of mind right now. There are many other ways to search for meaning in life. Whatever path you choose to travel, the key is to keep an open mind and a seeking heart.

RESOURCES

World Religions: The Great Faiths Explored and Explained, by John Bowker

A World of Faith, by Peggy Fletcher Stack and Kathleen B. Peterson

Finding Your Religion, by Rev. Scotty McLennan

The World's Wisdom: Sacred Texts of the World's Religions, by Philip Novak

Spiritual Literacy: Reading the Sacred in Everyday Life, by Frederic and Mary Ann Brussat

For more information on world religions visit:
www.religioustolerance.org

The Never-Ending Journey

One of my favorite songs by Joni Mitchell is called "The Arrangement." It is about a man who achieves great things throughout his life and accumulates nearly every luxury his heart can desire, from a fancy office to a big swimming pool. However, as the song progresses, we come to realize that this man lives in constant discontent. He is imprisoned by his commercial successes and deprived of true fulfillment. Joni laments this imaginary guy's unhappiness, singing, "You could have been more than a name on the door . . . more than a credit card, swimming pool in the backyard!"

Maybe this man isn't so imaginary after all. Is it possible that he lives inside us all, to some extent? As we continue on our soul searching journey, we must keep our goals in mind, and try to remember that happiness is more than a moment in which we are handed a trophy, a test score, or a glowing compliment. If we rely on these types of pleasures to bring us fulfillment, our joys will be few and far between. Instead, we must try to view life as a train ride taking us through many glorious and unique places and learn to appreciate the stunning panoramic view along the way just as much as the various destinations we stop at.

You've made a lot of wonderful progress with the soul searching techniques in this book, and hopefully you've experienced some breakthroughs in self-understanding. However, the journey's not over yet. As long as we're alive, we'll always have new opportunities to learn and grow; our souls have infinite room for expansion. The challenge you face now is to apply the discoveries you've made to your daily life long after you close this book's cover. How can we live up to our soul searching potential? Well, I've got three final secrets to share with you that can help you stay on the soul-searching path: assertiveness, goal setting, and positive affirmations.

What do YOU think?

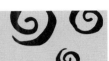

Sometimes it is [hard to stand up for your beliefs]. I think that's true for most of us. For example, it's hard to say to a guy I like "That's totally sexist!"

—LIZA BIRNBAUM, AGE 12

Some of my views on politics differ from those of people I know, but it has never really been an issue. I remind myself that people are not defined by their beliefs, they define their beliefs.

—JULIA HALPRIN JACKSON, AGE 16

Standing up for myself is something I hardly ever do. Sometimes I forget that my beliefs and opinions are as important as everyone else's.

—TANYA COLLINGS, AGE 14

I am very opinionated and sometimes I can feel uncomfortable standing up and debating. But if I strongly disagree with someone, or if I think what they are doing or saying is cruel and bigoted, I won't hesitate to tell them my stance.

—GILLIAN McHALE, AGE 15

I guess it's just a typical teenage impulse, but I love the look in people's eyes when I stand up for myself, and defend what I believe is right. It's rebellion, but with a just and moral bent to it.

—CAITLIN DWYER, AGE 16

ASSERTIVENESS: SPEAK YOUR MIND!

Now that you've figured out your passions and beliefs, it's time for the hard part—standing by your convictions. Too many young women I know shy away from starting debates or raising their hands in class, since girls are often taught to avoid controversy and conflict. In fact, upon entering adolescence, many of us become embarrassed by good grades or impressive achievements and try to hide them in fear of looking like a "goody-goody." As one teenage girl pointed out in *Reviving Ophelia*, "When I started junior high I figured out that I'd have more friends if I focused on sports. Smart girls were nerds."

Well, I've got news for you: smart girls aren't nerds anymore! Smart girls, by *my* definition, are magnetic and entertaining personalities who have faith in themselves, rely on their principles, and realize how to get things done. Smart girls are soul searchers. Yet even as a soul searcher you'll probably feel pressure to conform. Some people might even be intimidated by the power of your convictions. *In spite of this, you must learn how to resist conformity if you wish to stay true to yourself.* Even if your opinions are unpopular, people will admire your spunk and respect your individual voice, though they may not tell you that to your face.

Just by soul searching we are choosing to be a part of that rare breed who swim against the stream of popular opinion. In addition to this, we may also oppose the mainstream in other ways: we might dress differently, have unpopular political beliefs, believe in different gods, laugh too loud, or speak up when others don't. These things are parts of our identities, which we must come to embrace. Never force yourself into the wrong mold just to avoid being singled out. Sure, it's tempting to sacrifice your authenticity in order to impress boys, look good, or be considered "cool." But you must ask yourself what you value more, acceptance from others or your own integrity?

GOAL SETTING: SEIZE THE FUTURE IN YOUR HANDS!

We've only got one lifetime (unless you're a Hindu!), and we've got to milk it for all it's worth. As soon as we've discovered our true passions and our desires, the next logical step is making these dreams come true. How? In my experience, goal setting is the perfect way to turn lofty aspirations into more bite-sized objectives.

The first step in goal-setting is placing what we really want at center stage and pushing other people's hopes aside for the moment. Throughout our lives, we've been told (by parents, friends, relatives, teachers, and even society as a whole) who we ought to be and what we ought to want. Have you ever felt pressure from your dad to be a sports superstar? Or has your older sister made you feel like you'll never measure up? Goal-setting is the perfect time to break free of these chains and validate your own desires. What do you expect from life? What is going to make you happy? Who do you want to become?

Every once in a while I try to sit down with my journal and come up with a few goals for myself. Sometimes the things I write are vague and grandiose: *I want to travel the world, fly a plane, sing in a famous band.* Even if it seems ridiculous, it's important to dream big. Let your mind wander in a place where your future seems glorious, your job feels exciting, and the scenery looks magical and poetic. Get in touch with the basic yearnings of your soul—those things

Quiz: Do You Speak Your Mind?

Being assertive is a vital skill, even when it comes to the small things in life. If you can't muster enough courage to ask for a raise in your allowance, how can you hope to face larger issues like racism or drug abuse? Learning to be assertive in minor situations builds the confidence you'll need for more demanding confrontations. Take this quick quiz to see how your assertiveness measures up.

1. You order a hamburger at McDonalds, but you open up the bag to discover none other than a fish fillet. What do you do?
   a) Walk up to the counter, politely hand back the fish fillet, and explain that you ordered a hamburger.
   b) Interrupt the customer in front of you as you thrust the fish fillet back at the cashier, saying, "Excuse me! You screwed up my order. I'd like to talk to the manager!"
   c) Ask your friend to take it back for you. When she refuses, you shrug and eat it anyway.

2. Each week when your mom hands out the chore list, you notice that your responsibilities include cooking dinner, cleaning the bathroom, vacuuming, and dusting, while your oldest brother's only job is to take out the trash. This distribution seems unfair and even sexist to you, so:
   a) You tell your mom you would like to speak with her, and then calmly state your reasons for thinking that the chores are unfairly divided.
   b) You yell at your brother.
   c) You mutter under your breath, "This isn't really fair."

3. You know your boyfriend loves Rage Against the Machine, but you find them loud and obnoxious. When he turns on their new CD and asks what you think, you tell him:
   a) "I've never been a big fan of their music. Let's listen to Bob Marley instead."
   b) "Good God, this sucks! Turn it off."
   c) "Yeah, this music's really, um, cool."

Results:

Way to speak your mind! If you chose mostly A's, you're doing a good job of asserting your opinions in a friendly way. You understand the delicate balance between voicing your opinion and trampling on others.

Stop the steamroller. If you chose mostly B's, you're doing a good job of speaking your mind, which is great, but you sometimes do it at other people's expense. For example, you don't need to tell your boyfriend that his music "sucks" in order to let him know you'd prefer listening to something else.

Don't be a doormat. If you chose mostly C's, you probably have a hard time asserting yourself. Remember: you are a human being entitled to your own thoughts and opinions! While you might fear that people will reject you if you don't agree with them, this usually isn't the case. In fact, I've found some of my most rewarding friendships are with people who have very different opinions than my own. Although it's easier said than done, keep in mind that people who don't accept you for who you are generally are not worth your time.

you've always been afraid to admit wanting or haven't had the time for. What would you ask for if nothing was too exotic or outrageous to consider?

Other times, instead of writing far-off goals, I come up with a few basic and easily attainable ones. *Start taking voice lessons. Write a poem this morning. Do something nice for my stressed-out mom.* However small they may seem, these types of goals make it easier for me to conduct myself with purpose; they subtly add meaning to my day. Whenever life seems boring or pointless, try writing up a few simple aims for yourself.

Hold Onto Your Long-Term Goals

Along with lofty goals and simplistic ones, it's good to have some basic long-term aims to act as guideposts in our lives. Living spiritually, working hard academically, and excelling in athletics are good examples of long-term goals. Here are some guidelines to use when creating objectives like these:

Be dedicated. Don't give up on a goal when the going gets tough. You'll never experience satisfaction if you fling your dreams aside every time they seem boring or unattainable.

Be flexible. People change; goals change. Life is not as predictable as you might like it to be, which often means you'll have to readjust your expectations to fit reality.

Be stubborn, too. Certain goals are non-negotiable (integrity, for example). When it comes to your core values, you don't have to compromise for anyone.

Be happy. Celebrate your successes. When you reach a goal, take the time to rejoice and feel proud. For your smaller successes, make yourself a cup of hot cocoa or paint your toenails. For your big achievements, celebrate with a family dinner, a day of complete relaxation, or a slumber party with friends. Usually, the attainment of the goal is a reward in and of itself, but why miss a chance to celebrate?

Write Your Mission Statement

One of the most helpful goal-setting activities I know is writing a mission statement. When a new company is in the process of forming, the owners and employees may try to come up with a declaration of their goals and purpose, called

a "mission statement." The publishing company of this book, for example, has a mission
statement: "Inspire to Integrity." When the editors have a difficult decision to make about which
books to publish, they look to their mission statement
for guidance and ask "Will this book inspire people
to wholeness?" Members of the Army have a mis-
sion statement you're probably familiar with: "Be All That You Can Be." Simple
assertions like these keep our focus pointed in the right direction and help us
when we feel lost.

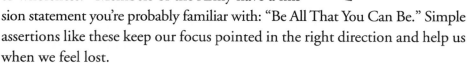

What exactly does a personal mission statement consist of? Well, it can be
formed in a variety of ways. Some people write just a sentence or two, others
write a paragraph, a page, or a list. You can quote a favorite author, philosopher, or song. Maybe you'll use a picture or a single word instead. Whatever
inspires you will do the job—it doesn't need to be original or profound.

My Mission Statement

When I first tried to write my own mission statement, I had a hard time getting it off the ground. I was striving for a perfect, Nobel Prize-worthy sentence
to base my life around, instead of just putting pen to paper. I realize now that
my mission statement is a work-in-progress. Even though I strive to keep the
core concepts intact, I'm always revising it and keeping it in touch with my life's
direction. As author Sean Covey points out in *The 7 Habits of Highly Effective
Teens*, "A personal mission statement is like a tree with deep roots. It is stable
and isn't going anywhere, but it is also alive and continually growing." Here's
what mine looks like right now:

Trust my intuition.
Try new things.
Listen.
Live with compassion.
Push myself.
Value integrity.
Thirst for knowledge.
Love as much as possible.
Enjoy.

Now it's your turn. If you're still at a loss for words, start paying attention to the things you value throughout your day. Read a book of quotes or listen more closely to the song lyrics you hear on the radio. Ask your parents and friends if they've ever used mission statements in their lives. If all else fails, just sit down and write whatever comes into your head. When your statement is complete, place it somewhere visible (on your computer, notebook, or mirror) and look at it whenever you need inspiration.

AFFIRMATIONS: BOOST YOUR THOUGHT POWER!

In elementary school, my teacher Ms. Mosher established a lovely tradition to start the day. All of us would gather in a circle and recite an affirmation: "I am beautiful. I am capable. I am lovable." When she first introduced the idea, we responded unanimously with giggles and smirks. "*I am beautiful.* . .is it okay to say that out loud?" I remember wondering to myself.

Soon, I learned that it was okay. Not only was it okay, it was magical to hear eleven young voices chanting such powerful phrases in unison. I'll never forget the strength and eloquence left reverberating in the room whenever we were done.

We can use affirmations in our daily lives to boost our creativity and confidence; they can also help us solidify our goals by keeping them at the forefront of our thinking. What exactly are affirmations? They tend to be short, succinct sentences that state a positive fact about our lives, or at least something we desire to be true.

Have you noticed how easily the average human mind can create negative thoughts and images? Do you ever feel powerless in the struggle against such negativity? That's where affirmations come to the rescue. They shower us with optimism and poise by exchanging destructive thoughts with constructive ones. For example, whenever I hear myself insulting my body or feeling self-conscious about it, I replace these thoughts with the phrase: *My body is healthy, beautiful, and strong. It serves me well.*

Affirmations work best when repeated frequently and out loud. Although it's good to recite them internally while standing in line at the movies or brushing your teeth, you'll add to their power by saving them for more sacred, silent moments. For instance, some people stand in front of the mirror upon waking, stare at themselves, and boldly declare their affirmations.

Because we've been taught to deny our virtues for the sake of "humility," it will probably feel awkward or even insane reciting affirmations for the first time. But the more you use them, the more you'll appreciate the infusion of comfort and confidence that they bring. Be patient. And remember that an affirmation doesn't have to be something that is true right now. It is incredibly powerful to assert something you *want* to be true in the future. Just that act alone can help make it come true.

Are you ready to give it a try? Here are ten simple affirmations to recite to yourself as often as you can:

1. I am happy, healthy, wise, and free.
2. Peace surrounds me in everything I do.
3. I am creative and talented.
4. I can release the past and forgive.
5. I listen to my own inner wisdom. With my intuition by my side, I am safe.
6. Everywhere I turn, I see potential for growth and opportunity.
7. I can be kind and assertive at the same time.
8. I am intelligent and I enjoy learning every day.
9. I have the capacity to love and be loved.
10. It is safe to look inside myself and discover my own opinions and beliefs. I am wise and beautiful. I love what I see in me. (This one is my personal favorite!)

WHERE DO WE GO FROM HERE?

Hopefully, you've made some discoveries inside the pages of this book. You deserve a pat on the back for your commitment to self-exploration. The techniques you've learned, from dream interpretation to prayer, are your personal "Keys to the Kingdom." And as I'm sure you've found, the Kingdom of Yourself is an astonishing place. When you know yourself, you'll be able to let your inner voice guide you in the right direction, *always*. We are constantly advancing and changing, which is why soul searching is a never-ending pursuit offering limitless rewards.

Of course, being a teenage girl isn't easy. Opportunities for growth and change aren't easily packaged. We learn from things like disaster and heartache. We mature from the unexpected, unpredictable, exciting, and painful events in our lives. We find strength out of sadness. At the same time, we can accelerate the process of growth using our own conscious efforts, which is what soul searching is all about.

There will certainly be roadblocks along the path to self-discovery. I can remember times when I thought I knew exactly what I was doing, only to realize I was completely wrong! I can remember times when I've hurt others, or let others hurt me. I can recall mistake after mistake—but most importantly, I'm learning from life and so are you!

When it all comes down to it, learning to love and appreciate ourselves is one of the most important things we'll ever do in our lives. When we meet the challenge of exploring our own depths, we'll be graced with a beauty we never knew existed. So instead of trying to hide from ourselves, let's keep searching our souls. Let's ask questions. Let's be patient and forgiving. Let's know our passions. Let's discover our mission in life and go get it. As a fellow soul searcher, I'm holding you in my heart and wishing you the best of luck!

Hey Soul Searchers!

Now that you've read book, get the journal!

Need a place to record your innermost thoughts?

Looking for creative and fun writing ideas?

Want to discover more about your dreams... your wishes... yourself?

Then the *Soul Searching Journal* is for you! This companion journal has tons of great soul searching ideas to spark your creativity. You can record your dreams, write your mission statement, and even collage your future. It's the perfect place to discover your true voice—and let your soul soar!

100 pages, 2-color illustrations, $10.95 hardcover spiral-bound

Other Books by Beyond Words Publishing

HEY, GIRLS! SPEAK OUT • BE HEARD
BE CREATIVE • GO FOR YOUR DREAMS

Discover how you can:
- handle grouchy, just plain ornery adults
- pass notes in class without getting caught
- avoid life's most embarrassing moments

✳ Scholastic & Book of the Month Club Selection ✳

Girls Know Best celebrates girls' unique voices and wisdom.
38 girls, ages 7-15, share their advice and activities. Everything you need to know...from the people who've been there: girls just like you!

160 pages, black and white collage art, $8.95 softcover

LISTEN UP!
GIRLS HAVE MORE TO SAY!

More girl wisdom on:
- how to have the best slumber party ever
- discovering the meanings of your dreams
- overcoming any obstacle, whenever, wherever

160 pages, black and white collage art, $8.95 softcover

GIRLS CANNOT BE SILENCED!
EVEN MORE GIRL TALK!

Answers all your questions about:
- different religions
- starting your own rock band
- whether alternative schooling is for you
  and, of course, much, much more!

132 pages, black and white collage art, $8.95 softcover

For a free catalog or to order books,
call Beyond Words Publishing 1-800-284-9673

HIS-STORY AIN'T THE WHOLE STORY

Did you know that:

- Joan of Arc was only 17 when she led the French troops to victory?
- Cristen Powell started drag racing at 16 and is now one of the top drag racers in America?
- Wang Yani began painting at the age of three? She was the youngest artist ever to have her own exhibit at the Smithsonian museum!

✳ Scholastic & Book of the Month Club Selection ✳

Girls Who Rocked the World lets you get to know these incredible teen-age girls and many more. This is the first book ever to set girls' history straight by telling the stories of inspiring young heroines.

120 pages, black and white art, $8.95 softcover

MORE GREAT STORIES OF REAL GIRLS WHO MADE HISTORY!

Impress your girlfriends with stories about:

- Hatchepsut, the first and only female Pharaoh, who ruled Egypt for more than twenty years.
- The Trung Sisters, who led Vietnam in a rebellion against foreign invaders almost 2000 years ago, winning independence for their country.
- Lauryn Hill, who rocked the music world with the Fugees at seventeen. Her solo album won her the most Grammys of any woman in history.

✳ A Troll Book Club Selection ✳

So . . . how are *you* going to rock the world? Both books include photos and essays from real girls about their plans for making history, just like their famous sisters.

160 pages, black and white illustrations, $8.95 softcover

For a free catalog or to order books,
call Beyond Words Publishing 1-800-284-9673

YOU GO GIRL!

Learn how to master your:
- Body: feeding and training your incredible machine
- Mind: talking yourself into sports success
- Spirit: dealing with others' negativity

Throw Like a Girl gives you information and inspiration to get involved in sports: for fun, for fitness, and even for a career. Hear from the experts, the stars, and from girls like you. Learn about sports nutrition and exercises while you're picking up tips for dealing with pushy coaches, teammates, and, oh yes, even parents.

160 pages, black and white collage art, $10.95 softcover

GROWING UP JUST GOT A LITTLE EASIER

Life can be tough, especially when you're in between everything. *The Girls Life Guide to Growing Up* helps relieve the stress of "tweendom" and "teendom" and shows you how to deal with:
- She's All That—Or is She?
  The myths of hangin' with the "in" crowd are busted by girls who have been there.
- What Kind of Smart Are You?
  Intelligence is more than a grade on a math test. This quiz reveals your true talents.
- Whose Body Is This, Anyway?
  Yeah, you're going through some crazy changes. Know what to expect and how to cope.

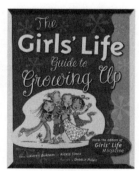

✳ Scholastic Book Club Selection ✳

It's as cool an advice book as you'll ever want, written by the staff of your favorite magazine, *Girls Life*. Take the quizzes, read the chapters and become self aware! See what guys really think about all this girl stuff, and laugh out loud as you read about everything girl, from friends, family, crushes, school, your body, and most of all, you!

272 pages, black and white illustrations, $11.95 softcover

**For a free catalog or to order books,
call Beyond Words Publishing 1-800-284-9673**

IS THERE A ROCK STAR IN THE HOUSE?

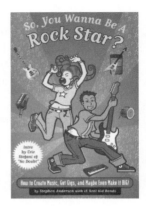

It could be you! All you budding musicologists, get the scoop on:

- Choosing the perfect name for your band
- Finding song ideas
- Creating a demo tape

✳ Scholastic & Book of the Month Club Selection ✳

How did Britney Spears get her start? This book won't tell you that, but it will inspire you to live your rock and roll dream: from how to start a band, to how to get discovered, and everything in between (like finding the perfect look and attitude to express your musical soul, and, of course, getting your parents on board to the whole idea of you as a rock star). Written by a former teenage rocker, with advice from twenty real kid bands. Rock on!

152 pages, black and white art, $8.95 softcover

DOES YOUR MEOWER HAVE PSYCHIC POWER?
DOES FIDO KNOW THINGS YOU DON'T KNOW?

Do you dare to explore the uncharted world of your pet's brain?

Read about:

- Spooky stories of pets with psychic powers
- Tests to find out if your pet is psychic
- Ways to increase your pet's psychic abilities
- Astrology charts for your pet

✳ Scholastic & Book of the Month Club Selection ✳

Can your cat get out of the house even when all the doors are closed? Has your dog ever seen a ghost? Does your horse seem to read your mind? If you can answer yes to any of these questions, you might have (are you sitting down?) a psychic pet! Better keep that food dish filled from now on!

124 pages, black and white art, $7.95 softcover

KIDSMAKINGMONEY.COM

Okay, *Better Than a Lemonade Stand* is not a guide to high tech riches. But computers aren't the only way to get rich quick. Learn how you can earn bucks by being a:

- baby-sitting broker
- dog walker
- mural painter

and many, many more fun money making jobs!!!

✳ Doubleday Book Club Selection ✳

Fifteen-year-old Daryl Bernstein started his first business when he was only eight. Since then, he has tried all fifty-one of the kid businesses in this book, all of which are easy to start up. Today, Daryl runs his own multi-million-dollar business and is happy to share with you the secrets of his success. Try on one of his entrepreneurial hats or let him inspire you to write your own rags to riches story!

150 pages, black and white cartoon illustrations, $9.95 softcover

EXCUSES! EXCUSES!

Authors Mike and Zach are excuse experts. These nine and ten year-old best friends have created *100 Excuses for Kids*, a hysterical book which will give you great excuses for getting out of anything—vegetables, homework, chores—whatever!

Get the latest and newest excuses for:

- Going to bed late
- Not eating your vegetables
- Not cleaning your room

and many (97 to be exact), many more

✳ Scholastic Book Club Selection ✳

"Dear Mike and Zach, My whole class loves your book! I have an idea for an excuse not to do your homework in the car: "But Mom, it's homework, not *car*work!"

—Blakeney, age 10

96 pages, black and white cartoon art, $5.95 softcover

**For a free catalog or to order books,
call Beyond Words Publishing 1-800-284-9673**

TO ORDER ANY OF THE BOOKS LISTED HERE OR TO REQUEST CATALOG, PLEASE CONTACT US OR MAIL US THIS ORDER FORM.

Name _____

Address _____

City _____ State/Province _____ Zip/Postal Code _____

Country _____

Phone Number _____

Title	Quantity	Price	Line Total

Subtotal _____

Shipping (see below) _____

Total _____

We accept Visa, MasterCard, and American Express, or send a check or money order payable to Beyond Words Publishing.

Credit Card Number _____ Exp. Date _____

Shipping Rates (within the United States only)
First book: $3.00   Each additional book: $1.00
Please call for special shipping services (overnight or international).

Beyond Words Publishing, Inc.
20827 NW Cornell Road, Suite 500
Hillsboro, OR 97124-9808

or contact us by phone: 1-800-284-9673
in Oregon (503) 531-8700
fax: (503) 531-8773
email: sales@beyondword.com